I0132700

Of Mudcat, Boo, The Rope and Oil Can …

An Informal History of Mississippians in Major League Baseball

Mike Christensen

SARTORIS
LITERARY
GROUP

A traditional publisher
with a non-traditional approach to publishing

Copyright ©2014 by Mike Christensen
Cover Design: Godfrey Jones

All rights reserved. WARNING: Unauthorized
duplication or downloading is a violation of
applicable laws, including U.S. Copyright law.
File sharing is allowed only with those companies
with which James L. Dickerson or Sartoris
Literary Group has a written agreement.

SARTORIS LITERARY GROUP
P.O. Box 4185
Brandon, MS 39047
www.sartorisliterary.com

To the memory of my great-grandfather Lawrence "Papa" Marshall and my dad, Wiggo "Chris" Christensen

Contents

Chapter 5: Powerball, 1995-Present

Introduction

On a Wednesday afternoon at Boston's South End Grounds, with the bases full of hometown Beaneaters, Cleveland Spiders outfielder Sport McAllister settled under a fly ball.

And dropped it.

Three runs scored. Cheers and jeers came from the well-oiled crowd of some 1,800. McAllister, a 24-year-old native of Austin, Mississippi, already was used to this kind of abuse.

It was May 31, 1899, and the worst season in major league baseball history was well under way. The Spiders lost that game 16-10. A week later, against the New York Giants, McAllister made two errors at third base. His teammates made nine.

Why was this happening? He had to wonder.

McAllister, in his fourth year with the National League club, was valued for his versatility on the field, but that seemed irrelevant. In fact, it almost made things worse as the losses piled up for the pitiful Spiders.

McAllister pitched in a game in mid-July and got shelled for five runs in one inning, taking the loss. He committed a comical passed ball as the catcher in a rare August home game before his own fans, and then made three errors as the third baseman in a 20-2 loss at Brooklyn's Ebbets Field a few days later. There was nowhere to hide.

On October 15, the season's final day, he pitched the opener of a doubleheader at Cincinnati's League Park and the Spiders lost 16-1. They lost Game 2 by 19-3. Cleveland's club—the Misfits, as they came to be known—finished 20-134. McAllister put up a .237 batting average. His ERA was 9.56. A lesser man might have given up the game right then and there.

Sport did not.

~ ~ ~

Who was the first Mississippi native to play modern major league baseball?

That's how this book got started—from just a little curiosity. Some research in *The Sports Encyclopedia: Baseball* produced the name of Lewis William "Sport" McAllister, born in Austin, Mississippi, in 1874. I had never heard of him, so I did some more digging into McAllister's history—and then into the background of other Mississippi-born players from the early years of the 20th century. Buried treasures began to emerge. A project was born.

Mississippians had a curious connection to Babe Ruth, widely considered baseball's greatest star. Mississippians influenced the career of Jackie Robinson, who broke the major leagues' color barrier in 1947.

Mississippians were involved in some of baseball's most memorable games and played on some of its most unforgettable teams.

There have been All-Stars, yes, but also many who barely shined at all. The Magnolia State has produced its share of colorful characters in the game and some of the best nicknames baseball has known. One of the sport's preeminent broadcasters was a Mississippi native.

The state also has strong traditions in college baseball and minor league baseball, both of which have funneled scores of players to the major leagues. This book touches on them, too, but the primary focus is Mississippi natives in the majors and how they fit into the fabric of major league history.

It's an overview, drawing from other published works as well as personal interviews and insights, a project that seemingly needed to be done.

There are a lot of statistics recited in this book, not without reason. Dyed-in-the-wool baseball fans love their stats. A player's numbers, put into context of team and season, can tell much about him even if little else is known. Stats welcome imagination. There's an image of a .290 hitter, of a pitcher with a 4.50 ERA. A 20-home run season tells you something.

For the purposes of organization, the book is divided into five chapters, each encompassing a so-called era of major league baseball.

Those are the deadball era of 1901-1919, the Babe Ruth era of 1920-45, the age of integration from 1946-1960, the expansion era of 1960-94 and the period some call "the steroid era," which began around 1995. Mississippians are presented against the backdrop of their times.

Sidebars accompany each chapter, highlighting such things as Mississippi natives in the World Series and in the old Negro Leagues. The closing sidebar tells the compelling—and very different—stories of three players who debuted in the big leagues in 2010.

Baseball is like no other sport. You don't have to be big or fast to play. It's not violent, not controlled by a clock. Kids and old-timers alike can take part.

Baseball has a history like no other sport and it celebrates its history like no other sport. Baseball's past is a portal into eternity. In these pages, one can be reminded of the parts, large and small, played by Mississippians in the long history of this grand old game.

**Pleasant Grove native Willie Mitchell
pitched in 276 games and won 83**

Chapter 1

Breaking In
1901-1919

A Team For All-Time

They might not scare off the 1927 Yankees—the iconic great team in Major League Baseball history—but an all-time, all-star club of Mississippi-born big leaguers certainly could hold its own on any fantasy field of play.

The Magnolia State can roll out five pitchers who won 20 or more games in a season, three batting champions, two home runs champs and a bushel of Gold Glove winners. And if we are allowed to dip into the old Negro Leagues, the man who likely would have set all kinds of stolen base records would also suit up for the Mississippi stars.

On this field of dreams, you could see Guy Bush handcuffing hitters with his fastball ... George Scott pounding homers to the deepest part of any ballpark ... Buddy Myer smacking singles to all fields or gobbling up grounders at shortstop ... Chet Lemon chasing down fly balls in center field with the speed and grace of a gazelle.

Here's a starting line-up you could win with:

Leading off and playing center field: Chet Lemon of Jackson, who hit .273 with 215 home runs and 58 stolen bases and set several records with his glove over a

15

16-year major league career. Starkville native Cool Papa Bell would fill this spot if we consider the Negro Leagues as major league, which is not a stretch. Bell was reputedly the fastest baseball player ever. He hit .341 in a 25-year Negro Leagues career, batted .391 against major league competition in exhibition games and stole 175 bases in one 200-game stretch.

Batting second, playing shortstop: Buddy Myer of Ellisville, the 1935 American League batting champion and a career .303 hitter. Myer came up as a shortstop before moving to second base, where he spent most of his 17 big league seasons.

Hitting third in right field: Dave Parker, born in Calhoun City, a .290 career hitter with 339 home runs. Parker played 19 years in the majors, won two batting crowns and was the 1978 National League Most Valuable Player.

The cleanup batter and first baseman: Greenville's George Scott, a.k.a. Boomer, who hit 271 homers in a 14-year major league career and won the American League homer and RBI titles in 1975.

Batting fifth in left field: Ellis Burks of Vicksburg, who played 18 years in the majors and batted .291 with 352 homers. His 1996 numbers — .344, 40 homers, 128

RBIs, 142 runs—amounted to one of the great offensive seasons of all-time.

In the six spot, at third base: Bill Melton, a Gulfport native who socked 160 homers in 10 seasons and won the American League home run title in 1971. Hattiesburg native Charlie Hayes, who hit .262 with 144 homers, would vie for time at third base, as well.

Batting seventh and playing second base: Frank White, born in Greenville, a .255 career hitter who drove in 886 runs and won eight Gold Gloves over 19 years. He helped Kansas City win a world title in 1985.

In the eighth spot, the catcher: Jake Gibbs, from Grenada, who batted .233 with 25 homers in a big league career spent entirely with the New York Yankees of the late 1960s and early 1970s. Gibbs could share this job with Yazoo City's Jerry Moses, who batted .251 in a nine-year career starting in the mid-'60s, or Barry Lyons, a Biloxi native who hit .239 as a journeyman backstop beginning in the mid-'80s.

Pitching and batting ninth … well, here's where you can get a great debate going. Who is Mississippi's all-time ace?

A strong case could be made for Guy Bush of Aberdeen, the "Mississippi Mudcat," who went 176-136 with a 3.86 ERA in a 17-year major league career from 1923-45.

But also worthy of consideration as Number 1 starter is Waynesboro native Claude Passeau, a 162-game winner who posted a 3.32 ERA from 1935-47.

Then there's Weir's Roy Oswalt, who arrived in the majors in 2001 and had 159 wins through 2011 to go with a 3.21 ERA. He was a three-time All-Star, won an ERA title and was 5-2 in postseason games. Boo Ferriss of Shaw (65-30, 3.64 ERA in an injury-shortened career that ran from 1945-50) and left-hander Reb Russell of Jackson (81-59, 2.34 from 1913-23) rate mention.

However you might rank them, it's a heckuva rotation.

Out in the bullpen, Hickory's Joe Gibbon (61 wins, 32 saves) and Chad Bradford of Byram (3.26 career ERA, 0.34 ERA in 24 postseason appearances) would provide capable relief — if any was ever needed.

On the bench, the Magnolia State dream team could have Gee Walker of Gulfport, a .294 career hitter; Pascagoula's Harry Walker, an National League batting champion; versatile infielders Don Blasingame of Corinth and Eric McNair from Meridian; power-hitting Luke Easter of Jonestown (93 homers in a brief big league career); and the ultimate situational player, Belzoni native Herb Washington, a onetime track star who served exclusively as a pinch runner for the Oakland A's in the mid-1970s.

Get Ellisville's Harry Craft, the first manager of the Houston Colt .45s (now Astros), to run the club and bring on those 1927 Yankees.

Breaking In

A total of 14 Mississippi-born players appeared in major league games in the first two decades of what is known as the modern era. These were the rough-and-tumble dead ball years, marked by "the scurrying of feet," as *The Sports Encyclopedia: Baseball* so vividly describes the period. The end of this era was brought about by the bat of one Babe Ruth, perhaps the game's most famous player and one with whom four Mississippians are inextricably linked.

In the popular 1989 film *Field of Dreams*, Ray Kinsella and Terence Mann take a trip to Minnesota in search of a ballplayer named Moonlight Graham, who played in one major league game, with the 1905 New York Giants, but never got to bat. They find that Graham is dead, but Kinsella is magically transported back in time and has a talk with Graham about his brush with the major leagues.

There actually was a Moonlight Graham, and he actually played in only one career game. But his experience was not unique. Two Mississippi natives — Howard "Lefty" Merritt of Plantersville and Pat McGehee of Meadville — also had one-game careers in the deadball era. They, too, have taken their stories to the grave. Unlike Ray Kinsella, we can't go back in time to pick their brains, but we do know a few facts.

Merritt, an outfielder, made his one appearance for the New York Giants on Sept. 27, 1913, at age 18. That Giants team, managed by legendary John McGraw, won the National League pennant with a roster that included Christy Mathewson, Rube Marquard, George Burns and Fred Merkle. Shades of Moonlight Graham, Merritt didn't even get to bat in his one game. McGehee, a right-handed pitcher, started a game on Aug. 23, 1912, for the Detroit Tigers, a club that included Ty Cobb and Sam Crawford. Statistics show that McGehee faced two batters, allowing a hit and a walk. He then left the game, and his major league career was over at age 23. He's a virtual ghost in the record books, with zero innings pitched and no ERA.

Ray Roberts of Cruger and Phil Redding of Crystal Springs avoided the Moonlight syndrome—but ever so narrowly. Roberts pitched in three games for the 1919 Philadelphia Athletics, a Connie Mack-managed team that is recognized as one of the worst of all-time. The A's went 36-104, and Roberts, a right-hander, contributed an 0-2 record and a 7.71 ERA in 14 innings. Redding, also a righty, spread his thin career over two seasons. He was 2-1 in three starts for the 1912 St. Louis Cardinals and made one three-inning appearance with the same club the next year.

~ ~ ~

Baseball in the first two decades of the modern era was quite different from the game we watch today. One can imagine, say, the atmosphere at old Shibe Park in Philadelphia, where Cruger's Roberts pitched for those awful 1919 A's. At that time, the park seated 20,000. It sat on the corner of 21st Street and Lehigh Avenue in downtown Philadelphia. A French Renaissance church-like dome that housed the main entrance made the park an unmistakable landmark. Fans who lived on 20th Street could sit on their roofs and watch the game over a 12-foot high fence in right field.

Fans, or cranks, as they were commonly called in those days, would often ride to the games in streetcars pulled by horses. The stadiums in many cases were just glorified grandstands with (sometimes) a fence around the playing area. Spectators frequently spilled onto the field itself. Outfield dimensions were typically huge; it was 502 feet to dead center field in Shibe Park.

Prior to 1911, the ball was so dead it practically cried out for a life-support system. Pitchers could legally throw the spitter, and the same ball often remained in play for the entire game. Hitters were at a major disadvantage. Even a well-struck ball might not have reached the outfield, much less left the park. Managers played for one run, calling for bunts and stolen bases, hunting and pecking to put up numbers on the hand-operated scoreboards. Even after the cork-center ball was introduced in 1911, pitchers still dominated. Batting averages rose, but home runs still were not a prominent part of the game.

The players in those days were a disparate group, not nurtured, coddled, millionaire athletes like we see today. They were "more colorful, drawn from every walk of life. We had stupid guys, smart guys, tough guys, mild guys, crazy guys, college men, slickers from the city and hicks from the country," Davy Jones, an outfielder with the Detroit Tigers of the dead ball era, said in Lawrence Ritter's *The Glory of Their Times.*

All the players had a hard edge; they needed it. "Baseball is something like a war," the great Ty Cobb once said. "Baseball is a red-blooded sport for red-blooded men. It's not pink tea, and mollycoddles had better stay out of it. It's … a struggle for supremacy, a survival of the fittest."

This was the world in which Mississippians like Sport McCallister, Pete Shields, Dode Criss, Willie Mitchell, Sammy Vick, Reb Russell and others tried to earn their keep.

Players of that era should be genuinely admired. They played for the love of the game and not much more. Before Babe Ruth became a star in New York in the 1920s, nobody got rich playing baseball, not even the gamblers and cheats who infiltrated some clubs. There were no long-term contracts, no big endorsement deals. Many of the players were farmers who returned to their fields in the off-season. Others held down regular jobs to make ends meet.

~ ~ ~

Of all the Mississippi-born players who toiled in those hardscrabble days, Willie Mitchell, a left-handed pitcher from Sardis (or Pleasant Grove in some reference books) probably enjoyed the best sustained career. He appeared in 275 games in an 11-year span, going 84-92 with a 2.86 ERA. He came up with Cleveland of the American League in 1909 and pitched for the Indians until 1916, when he was traded to Detroit. He never played for a pennant winner.

Mitchell struck out 921 hitters in his career, but one stands out. On July 11, 1914, while facing the Boston Red Sox at Fenway Park, Mitchell struck out a rookie pitcher in his first big league at-bat. That pitcher was Babe Ruth. Ruth and the Red Sox went on to win the game, the first of many Ruth would win before he was traded to the New York Yankees and became a fulltime, record-breaking slugger.

Mitchell went 12-8 with a 2.59 ERA in 1910, his second major league season. His best year likely was 1913, when he posted a 14-8 mark and a 1.74 ERA (second in the AL to Walter "Big Train" Johnson) and helped the Indians go 86-66, good for third place. The club fell to 51-102 in 1914, but Mitchell hung up a 13-17 record and struck out 179 batters (second in the league to

Johnson). Mitchell went 12-8, 2.19 with Ty Cobb's Tigers in 1917, his last full year in the majors. He pitched just one game in 1918 because of military duties and made three starts in 1919.

Jackson native Ewell Albert Russell, a.k.a. Reb, actually had two big league careers. The first began in 1913, when he won 22 games as a rookie left-hander for the Chicago White Sox, and ended in 1919, when he came down with a dead arm. Russell's second career started in 1922, when he came back for a two-year stint as an outfielder for the Pittsburgh Pirates.

Russell was with the White Sox during their rise as an American League powerhouse. He left just before the team's fall in the 1919-20 Black Sox scandal that threatened to destroy the credibility of baseball.

In 51 appearances in 1913, Russell went 22-16 with four saves and a 1.91 ERA for a fifth-place team. Russell won eight games the next year as the ChiSox finished sixth, 11 games in 1915 as the team rose to third place and 17 in 1916 for a club that finished second to Boston by two games.

Most of the eight so-called Black Sox, including Shoeless Joe Jackson, were on the team by 1917, when Chicago won the American League pennant and beat the

New York Giants in the World Series. Russell was the No. 4 starter that season and went 15-5 with a 1.94 ERA. He started Game 5 of the World Series but was knocked out in the first inning.

Arm problems limited Russell to 19 games in 1918 and one brief appearance in 1919. He wasn't with the club that fall when the Black Sox conspirators threw — or allegedly threw — the World Series against Cincinnati.

In 1922, at age 33, Russell enjoyed a rebirth. The game had changed by that time. Babe Ruth's popularity as a home run basher had induced the baseball powers to opt for a livelier ball and to outlaw the spitter and other doctored pitches. Russell, playing in just 60 games for a Pittsburgh club that included Pie Traynor and Max Carey, hit .368 with 12 homers and 75 RBIs. Russell added nine more homers in 1923, his final season in the majors.

~ ~ ~

Most of the Mississippians who broke in during the deadball days had the misfortune to play for bad teams. The dominant clubs of the 1901-19 period were the Chicago Cubs, Philadelphia Athletics and Boston Red Sox, all with five pennants apiece, and the New York

Giants, who won four. There were no Mississippians on any of those teams.

Austin native Sport McAllister, the first Mississippi-born player in the modern era, played on the worst major league team of all-time, the 1899 Cleveland Spiders. Ray Roberts' brief season with the A's came after owner-manager Connie Mack purged the team of most of its stars and turned it into a lousy outfit. Pete Shields of Swiftwater was a first baseman—and a teammate of Willie Mitchell's—on the 1915 Indians, a seventh-place team in an eight-team circuit. That was Shields' only year in the big leagues; he hit .208 in 23 games.

Holly Springs' Red Smyth, an outfielder who also played some at second and third base, was a rookie with the 1915 Brooklyn Dodgers when they finished third. The next season, the Dodgers won the National League pennant, but Smyth batted only five times that year and wasn't on the World Series roster. The Dodgers collapsed in 1917, and Smyth was traded to the St. Louis Cardinals, for whom he batted .208 as they finished third. In 1918, despite the emergence of a young hitter named Rogers Hornsby, the Cardinals fell to last place. Smyth hit .212 in what was his final season.

Dode Criss of Sherman played in 227 big league games—all with the St. Louis Browns, a cursed franchise that would win its only American League pennant during World War II and ultimately move to Baltimore and become the Orioles. Criss, an outfielder who also did some pitching, hit .341 as a rookie in 1908 during one of the great American League pennant races. The Browns eliminated the Cleveland Naps on the next-to-last day of the season but finished fifth themselves, far off the pace of champion Detroit.

Ripley's Dolly Stark had the best of his four major league seasons in 1911, when he batted .295 in 70 games for Brooklyn. But that team was an awful 64-86. Stark would play just one more year.

Sammy Vick of Batesville and Slim Love, whose listed hometown is Love, played for the New York Yankees before that franchise took on its aura of greatness. In fact, the team wasn't yet playing in Yankee Stadium when this pair played in New York.

Love was a 6-foot-7, 195-pound left-hander—hence the nickname Slim—who began his six-year big league career in Washington and ended it in Detroit. He was 21-17 in three seasons with the Yankees (1916-18), this despite leading the American League in walks in

1918. Vick, an outfielder, played parts of four years with the Yankees (1917-20). Both were gone when Babe Ruth led the team to its first pennant in 1921 and launched the dynasty we know today.

Ruth's exploits as a swaggering slugger—he hit 714 career homers, a record that stood for almost 40 years — captured the fancy of baseball fans and might well have saved the game from ruin in the wake of the Black Sox mess. To be sure, Ruth turned the game on its ear.

The First ... and Worst

Mississippi native William Lewis McAllister clearly had a zest for baseball. In the early days of his professional career, the man they called "Sport" would "spend time warming up by bouncing balls against the grandstand and chasing them down like a kid dreaming of the pro league," J. Thomas Hetrick wrote in *Misfits: The Cleveland Spiders* in 1899.

McAllister played seven years in the major leagues, breaking in in 1896, bowing out in 1903. It's a wonder, really, that McAllister's enthusiasm for the game wasn't crushed in 1899, when he had the misfortune to wear the uniform of the Cleveland Spiders, the Ohio-based team generally recognized as the worst in major league history.

The '99 Spiders, who came to be called the Misfits, finished with a 20-134 record, 84 games out of first place in the 12-team National League. They were 35 games out of 11th place. They lost 40 of their last 41 games. The club's penny-pinching owner juggled the schedule and forced the Spiders to play 113 road games. They went 11-102. They finished last in the league statistics in batting, scoring, home runs and earned run average.

The 1962 New York Mets were a bad team, but they were laughable, lovable losers playing their first season in the National League. The '99 Spiders were just plain dreadful. Only 6,000 people saw them play at home, in Cleveland's League Park, the entire season. Writers in Cleveland and other cities ridiculed them in print and frequently called for the club to be dismissed from the league. One newspaper described their play as resembling "those bunch of colonial dames playing bean bag in the weedy back lot of an asylum for the feeble-minded."

In the middle of this mess was Sport McAllister.

He was born on July 23, 1874, in Austin, a speck of a town in Tunica County, tucked way up in the northwest corner of Mississippi. When baseball entered its so-called modern era in 1901 — that is, when the American League joined the National League as a "major league" — McAllister was the only Mississippi-born player on a roster in either league. He was the state's baseball pioneer. (It is worth noting that at least one other Mississippi native — Natchez-born Doug Crothers — played in the pre-1901 major leagues. Crothers, a pitcher, appeared in 21 games for the Kansas City Unions and the New York Metropolitans from 1884-85. He was 8-13 with a 4.63 ERA.)

McAllister grew up in Fort Worth, Texas, and played minor league ball in the Texas League. In 1896, he was signed by the Spiders of the National League, the country's premier circuit. He played only eight games that first year for a second-place team that featured future Hall of Fame pitcher Cy Young. The versatile McAllister, a switch-hitter who threw right-handed, played six different positions in 60 games for the Spiders over the next two seasons.

In 1899, Cleveland owner Frank Robison bought the St. Louis Browns, another National League franchise. Because St. Louis was a bigger city — and because it had no ban on playing on Sundays — Robison decided to move his best players from the Spiders to his new club, which he called the Perfectos. Cleveland was left with what was described as "a mix of over-the-hill incompetents and young non-prospects."

Even though he couldn't possibly have known how bad the Spiders would be, McAllister was disappointed to be assigned to Cleveland for the '99 season. He had trained that spring in Hot Springs, Ark., with the newly formed Perfectos and wanted to play in St. Louis.

Some accounts of McAllister's playing ability are not flattering. "Possessing little talent to excel in any one position," Hetrick wrote, "McAllister played them all. … Manager Pat Tebeau (the Spiders' skipper in McAllister's first three seasons) kept trying to find a position for the stocky, switch-hitting utilitarian. More likely, though, McAllister was a full-time fill-in, performing when other players were hurt or hung over."

Yet McAllister would demonstrate later in his career that he could be a capable big leaguer. In 1901, playing for the American League Detroit Tigers in their first season as a "major league" team, he hit .301 with three homers and 57 RBIs in 90 games. He did everything but pitch and play second base that year. In 1903, he was the Tigers' regular shortstop and batted .260 in 78 games.

But in 1899, with the Spiders, nothing went right. McAllister battled injuries much of the year but got into 113 games. He hit .237 with 31 RBIs. In three appearances as a pitcher, including the next-to-last game of the season (a 16-1 loss), he was 0-1 with a 9.56 ERA. He played every position on the field and committed 28 errors.

The National League dropped four teams from its organization after the 1899 season and the Spiders, mercifully, were one of them. The Cleveland players scattered far and wide. McAllister landed in Detroit and hit .306 for the Tigers in 1900. He stayed with the Tigers through the 1903 season, then played 13 more years in various minor leagues.

He died in Wyandotte, Michigan, on July 17, 1962. In *The Ballplayers*, a splendid biographical reference work published in 1990, he is cited for his versatility; there is no mention there of the Spiders or that season in hell, for which McAllister likely would have been very thankful.

Spotlight

And What of the Best?

In the book *Baseball Dynasties: The Greatest Teams of All Time*, authors Rob Neyer and Eddie Epstein agree that the best major league team was the 1939 New York Yankees, who dominated the American League and won the World Series in a four-game sweep. And, yes, there was a Mississippian on that club. Morton native Atley Donald, then in his second major league season, was 13-3 with a 3.71 ERA for the '39 Yanks.

That club, managed by Joe McCarthy, went 106-45 and won the American League pennant by 17 games over second-place Boston. The 1939 Yankees led the league in runs scored and fewest runs allowed, a remarkable feat. (That was also the season in which Lou Gehrig made his famous "luckiest man on the face of the earth" speech at Yankee Stadium.)

Joe DiMaggio was the best player on the team, batting .381 with 30 home runs and 126 RBIs. Three other players had 21 or more homers and 100 or more RBIs. Red Ruffing led the pitching staff with a 21-7 mark and a 2.93 ERA.

There were six double-digit winners all told. The Yankees outscored Cincinnati 20-8 in the 1939 World Series. Donald never even made an appearance. Donald would later gain some recognition as the scout who signed Ron Guidry, a.k.a. Louisiana Lightning, the ace of the Yankees' world championship clubs of 1977 and 1978.

Make Way for the Babe

One imagines that Sammy Vick returned from military service in 1919 ready and rarin' to play some ball. The Batesville native broke into the big leagues with the New York Yankees in 1917 but played in just 10 games. Military duties limited Vick to two games in the war-scrambled 1918 season.

In 1919, Vick was 24 and in his baseball prime, and it showed on the field. The 5-foot-10, 163-pound right-handed hitter became the Yankees' regular right fielder and leadoff batter that season. He played in 100 games alongside center fielder Ping Bodie and left fielder Duffy Lewis and hit .248 with two homers, nine triples, 27 RBIs and 59 runs. The Yankees finished third in the American League.

But fate was not kind to Vick in the months that followed. The Yankees acquired a portly left-handed pitcher-turned-hitter from the Boston Red Sox during the winter of 1920. Babe Ruth's arrival in New York for the 1920 season signaled the start of a glorious new era for baseball—and the beginning of the end for Sammy Vick.

Ruth took over in right field and hit 54 home runs in his first season in pinstripes. Vick played in 51 games

35

and batted just 116 times, hitting .220. He was the club's fifth outfielder behind Ruth, Bodie, Lewis and young Bob Meusel.

There were, from all indications, no hard feelings between Vick and the Babe. They hung out together during that first spring training in Jacksonville, Fla., and shared at least one talent. If Vick couldn't hit like Ruth, he could certainly eat like him.

The legendary writer Damon Runyan reported during the rain-drenched spring of 1920 that "Ruth and Vick already have the waiters at the Hotel Burbridge run flatfooted." Vick reputedly had such a reputation for eating that teammates referred to the consumption of a large meal as "doing a Sammy Vick." Stuck inside by rain, writers in Jacksonville with the team organized a Great All-American Table Stakes, in which Vick and Ruth were prominent participants.

Vick also claimed to be the only player to pinch hit for Ruth during the Babe's 15 years with the Yankees. Vick, who died in 1986, recounted the incident in a 1975 interview with The (Memphis) Commercial Appeal.

Vick said that Ruth had injured his arm during a game, and with the Yankees down three runs and the bases loaded, manager Miller Huggins called on Vick to pinch hit.

Vick said his mind went blank as he walked to the plate and heard the announcement: "Batting for Ruth, Sammy Vick." The next thing he remembered, Vick said, was sliding into third base with a game-tying triple. Vick's claim is difficult to substantiate.

Records show Vick did have a triple during the 1920 season, but in three books about Ruth, the pinch-hit incident is never mentioned.

Still, it makes for a good story and adds to the list of interesting connections between the legendary Sultan of Swat and Mississippi natives.

When the Yankees' dynasty "officially" began in 1921, the year the team won its first American League pennant, Vick was in Boston, with a Red Sox team that ran a distant fifth. He hit .260 in 44 games, even played catcher in one. But his career skidded off the big-league track the next year and he never made it back.

Jackson native Ewell Albert "Reb" Russell enjoyed success first as a pitcher and then as a hitter, 1913-1923

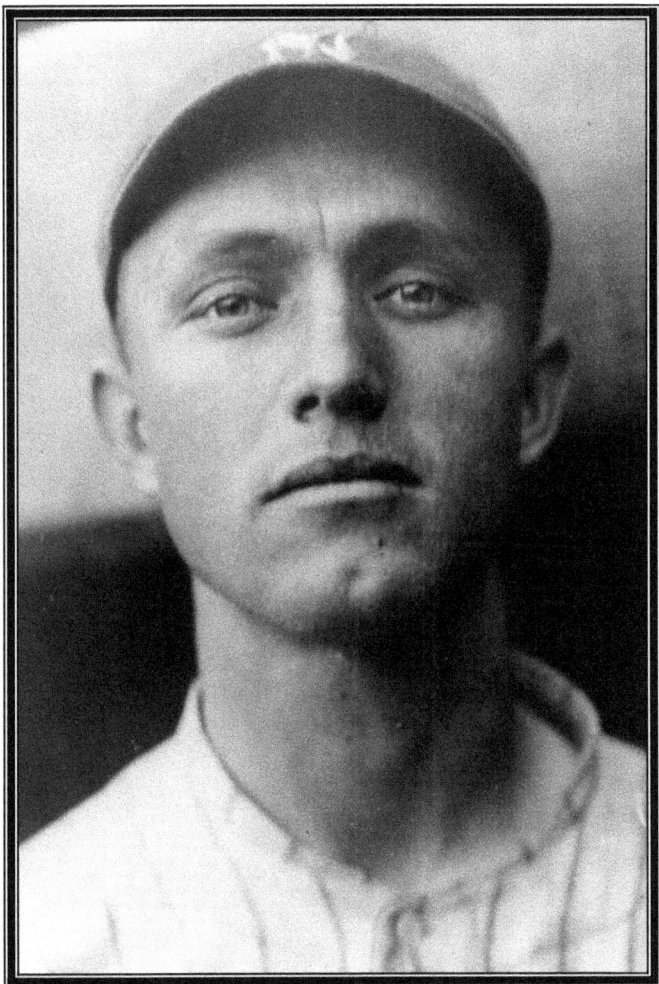

**Batesville native Sammy Vick broke in
with the Yankees in 1917 and played four more years**

Chapter 2

Bloomin' Magnolias
1920-1945

**Ellisville native Buddy Myer was a .303 hitter
and two-time All Star**

A Goodbye to Remember

The careers of Aberdeen native Guy Bush and the great Babe Ruth intersect at two points that are earmarked in baseball's history books.

Flash to October 1, 1932, Game 3 of the World Series, Wrigley Field, Chicago. Ruth, playing for the New York Yankees, hits the Called Shot, his storied home run off Cubs pitcher Charlie Root. But mystery surrounds the moment.

Did Ruth really predict his home run, or was he merely gesturing toward the Cubs' bench, toward Guy Bush, in particular?

Zoom in on May 25, 1935, Forbes Field, Pittsburgh. An ailing Ruth, playing his final season with the Boston Braves, hits three home runs, his last three, including a mammoth shot that left the stadium. Guy Bush served up the last two, Numbers 713 and 714 of the Babe's career.

In the first at-bat of his big league career, in 1914, Ruth struck out against Mississippi native Willie Mitchell. In 1920, after he was sold from the Boston Red Sox to the New York Yankees, Ruth displaced Mississippi native Sammy Vick in right field for the Bronx Bombers.

On May 30, 1935, in the last at-bat of his career, Ruth grounded out against Jackson native Jim Bivin. And most trivia experts will remember that Mississippi native Guy Bush served up Ruth's last two home runs;

they might also remember Bush for his association with the Called Shot.

But it would be a shame indeed if those were the only things Bush were remembered for. The Mississippi Mudcat, who died in 1986, put up career numbers that fell short of Hall of Fame caliber but are nonetheless impressive. Bush was 176-136 with a 3.86 ERA in a career that spanned 22 years. He first pitched in a big league game in 1923 at the age of 21, and he came back after a six-year layoff to pitch again in 1945, during the war years, at age 43.

The 6-foot, 175-pound right-hander won 152 games for the Cubs between 1923 and 1934, a celebrated era for a franchise known more today for its failures. In 1927, Bush pitched an 18-inning complete game against the Boston Braves. The next year, he went 15-6. In 1929, he led the National League with 50 appearances, saved eight games, won 18 and helped the Cubs take the pennant. Despite a lineup that included Hack Wilson, Kiki Cuyler and Gabby Hartnett, the Cubs lost the 1929 World Series to the Philadelphia Athletics 4-1. Bush got the Cubs' only win.

Bush went 15-10 despite a 6.20 ERA during the juiced-ball season of 1930 (when his teammate Wilson set the all-time RBI record with 190), posted a 16-8 mark in 1931 and a 19-11 record in 1932, when the Cubs went back to the World Series, this time to face Ruth and the Yankees.

Aberdeen native Guy Bush, known as the "Mississippi Mudcat," won 176 games over at 17-year career

The Yankees won the first two games in New York, beating Bush in the opener. There was bad blood in the Series from the start. Ex-Yankees infielder Mark Koenig had joined the Cubs in midseason and helped them win a tight National Leaguer pennant race. But the Cubs had voted Koenig just a half-share of the World Series bonus. The Yankees had learned of this and chided the Cubs about it.

A crowd of 51,000 packed Wrigley Field for Game 3, and the verbal jousting continued. When Ruth came to bat in the fifth inning, having already homered once off Charlie Root, the score was 4-4.

Ruth had misplayed a ball in right field in the fourth inning, allowing the tying run to score. The Cubs gave him an earful as he stood at the plate. "The Chicago bench jockeys were really letting (Ruth) have it; particularly Guy Bush, a pitcher with a raucous voice and a rich assortment of insults," Kal Wagenheim wrote in *Babe Ruth: His Life and Legend.*

Ruth apparently held up one finger when Root's first pitch was called a strike. After two balls, Root threw another strike, and Ruth held up two fingers. The shouting from the Cubs bench intensified, and Ruth stepped back and lifted a finger.

"Where he pointed is a subject of debate," Wagenheim wrote. "Cub catcher Gabby Hartnett claims (Ruth) waived his hand toward the Cub bench and yelled, 'It only takes one to hit it.' Lou Gehrig, who was kneeling a few feet away in the on-deck circle, says that Ruth pointed at Guy Bush in the dugout and yelled, 'I'm gonna cut the next pitch right down your—throat.' Pat Pieper, the Wrigley Field announcer, says Ruth pointed to center field. John Drebinger of the *New York Times* ... made no mention in his (game) story of Ruth's pointing, but he did say the Babe predicted a homer 'in no mistaken motions.'"

Bush claimed in later interviews that Ruth pointed toward the outfield — not at him.

Regardless, Root's fifth pitch to Ruth left the park in deep center field, out toward the corner of Waveland and Sheffield Avenues. Gehrig followed with a homer. The mighty Yankees won the game and then pounded Bush in Game 4 to sweep the Series. Bush hit Ruth with a pitch in the first inning off the final game, and the Babe allegedly laughed all the way to first base. Bush didn't make it out of the inning.

Bush won 20 games in 1933 and 18 in 1934, but the Cubs slipped to third place both years. He was traded to Pittsburgh in 1935 — the year the Cubs made it back to the World Series — and destiny carried him to another meeting with Ruth. On May 25. At Forbes Field.

The Pirates' starter that day was Red Lucas, and Ruth hit his first home run against him. Bush came on in relief and faced Ruth for the first time since the contentious 1932 Series.

Ruth was an old 40 and just eight days from the end of his playing career. Bush was 33 and on the downhill side of his career, as well, but he was making no concessions to Ruth on this day.

"I told Tommy Padden, our catcher, 'I'm gonna throw the ball by this big monkey,'" Bush recalled years later. It didn't get by him. Ruth's second homer of the day barely cleared the fence in right field, just 300 feet away in Forbes Field. "Is that the kind of home runs that big jackass has been hitting in the American League?" Bush said. Next time up, Bush again challenged Ruth with a fastball.

"He hit it out of the cockeyed park. Looked like it went to St. Louis," Bush would say. "I watched him all around the bases. He just hobbled around, couldn't hardly run. As he went around third base, I took my cap off and bowed to him. He just kind of nodded and smiled."

Ruth's last home run, some say, was the longest ever hit at Forbes Field, which was torn down in the 1970s. The ball cleared the right field roof, which was 86 feet high, and was the first of only 16 that would leave the park in that vicinity.

Bush finished 11-11 in 1935 and was traded by the Pirates to the Braves during the 1936 season. He was dealt again in 1938, to St. Louis, and appeared in only six games for the Cardinals. His war-time comeback with Cincinnati in 1945 lasted just four games, though he did record a save.

That finished off a career that should rate much more than a footnote or two in baseball's annals.

Bloomin' Magnolias

Baseball recovered from the Black Sox scandal and its popularity zoomed in this quarter century, a period that encompassed the fantastic rise of Babe Ruth and the Yankees, the woe of the Great Depression and the horror of World War II. A great wave of Mississippians, 43 by actual count, entered the major leagues during this time, including some of the state's enduring legends.

When Babe Ruth socked 54 home runs for the Yankees in 1920, his first season in New York, it clearly marked the end of an age of the pitcher. The wicked spitter was outlawed in 1921, and the ball became ever livelier. Batters began to use thin-handled bats (ala Ruth), which they could whip at the ball, increasing bat speed and power. Steel stadiums with smaller outfield dimensions had begun to spring up in the decade prior to 1920, and these were the standard by the mid-1920s. The first Yankee Stadium, the House That Ruth Built with its short right-field porch, went up in 1923. Home runs became the key to success, for hitters and teams.

But Mississippians, as they are wont to do, bucked the trend. The best hitters to come out of the Magnolia State in the era from 1920-45 weren't home run hitters.

Ellisville native Buddy Myer won a batting title with the Washington Senators in 1935, but he never hit more than six homers in a season. Gerald "Gee" Walker of Gulfport hit 124 homers in his 15 seasons but never more than 18 in any one year; he had many more stolen bases (223 career) than bombs. Sam Leslie of Moss Point was a career .304 hitter, but he hit just 36 homers in 10 seasons in the majors. Hughie Critz of Starkville, Ellisville's Harry Craft, Eric "Boob" McNair of Meridian … all were gap-to-gap hitters.

Pitchers in general may have had a tougher time during this period, but Claude Passeau of Waynesboro and Aberdeen native Guy Bush emerged as two of the best pitchers Mississippi has ever produced. And on the cusp of this era came a tall kid from the Delta named Dave Ferriss, another standout hurler.

Passeau went 162-150 with a 3.32 ERA in his 13 seasons and threw a brilliant one-hitter in the 1945 World Series for the Chicago Cubs. Bush, the "Mississippi Mudcat," was 176-136 with a 3.86 ERA over 17 seasons. He won 15 or more games in seven straight years during his prime.

Atley "Swampy" Donald, a hard-throwing righty from Morton, was a sparkling 65-33 with a 3.52 ERA in eight seasons with the mighty Yankees, who won five pennants during Donald's time with the club. Benn "Baldy" Karr of Mount Pleasant and Grenada native Ike Pearson each pitched more than 150 games in the big leagues, though both had the misfortune to work for some awful teams. Karr—who yielded the 10th of Ruth's 60 home runs in 1927—was 35-48 with a 4.60 ERA, pitching for Boston and Cleveland in the American League. Pearson was 13-50 with a 4.84 ERA in a six-year career spent mostly with the Philadelphia Phillies. Had either pitched for contending clubs, their records no doubt would have been better and their names more well-known.

~ ~ ~

James "Cool Papa" Bell and Bill Foster, stars of the old Negro Leagues, are the only native-born Mississippi players in the National Baseball Hall of Fame in Cooperstown, N.Y. You can make a pretty good argument that Buddy Myer should be in there, too.

Myer, a 5-foot-10, 150-pound left-handed hitter, was widely regarded as one of the best all-around second basemen of his day. He hit .303 for his 17-year career, won a batting title, won a stolen base title, played in two World Series with the Washington Senators, twice made the American League All-Star team, twice led American League second baseman in fielding and set a league mark for double plays by a second baseman.

Yet all of those notable accomplishments did not get Myer, who died in 1974, into the Hall of Fame. He got one vote in 1949. That's it. His fate rests with the Veterans Committee. "Buddy should have been in a long, long time ago," Harry Craft, a Myer contemporary in the big leagues and another Ellisville native, told *The Clarion-Ledger* newspaper in 1990.

Myer was recognized in the book *Baseball's Dream Teams* as an honorable mention selection among the 1930s-era second basemen: "Myer was a well-respected gloveman, but not a star like (Detroit's) Charlie Gehringer." *In Low and Outside*, a book about Depression-era baseball, William B. Mead writes of Myer: "Underappreciated in an era of power hitters, Myer also had to put up with flurries of anti-Semitism from opponents." Bill James' *Historical Baseball Abstract*, published in 2001, ranked Myer 24th among second baseman all-time, ahead of the likes of Johnny Evers, Bill Mazeroski, Mississippian Frank White, Eddie Stanky and Bobby Avila.

Myer was not a practicing Jew, though he was recognized on an all-Jewish team published by *The Sporting News* in 1935. He played at Mississippi A&M (now Mississippi State University) for Dudy Noble and entered pro ball with the minor league New Orleans Pelicans in 1924. The Senators bought his contract in 1925, and that October, at the age of 21, he was playing in the World Series.

In 1926, Myer batted .304 as the Senators' regular shortstop. During the 1927 season, Washington owner Clark Griffith traded Myer to the Boston Red Sox for Topper Rigney. Griffith later called it "the dumbest deal I ever made."

In 1928, Myer led the American League in stolen bases with 30 and hit .313. The following year, Griffith sent five players to Boston to get Myer back, and he was the Senators' regular second baseman for most of the next 10 years. He helped them to a World Series berth in 1933 and in 1935 put up MVP-type numbers: a league-best .349 average, 115 runs and 100 RBIs. Myer went 4-for-5 on the last day of the 1935 season to edge Cleveland's Joe Vosmick for the batting title. Detroit's Hank Greenberg, who slugged 36 homers and drove in 170 runs, won the MVP award.

An unspecified illness limited Myer to 51 games in 1936, but he bounced back with an All-Star year in 1937 and hit .336 the year after that. But in 1939, at age 35, he was displaced as the Senators' everyday second baseman by Jimmy Bloodworth. Myer continued to hit as a part-timer, batting .300 in '39, .290 the next year and .253 in 53 games in '41, his final season.

Myer was widely regarded as a gentleman off the field and a battler on it. George Case, a teammate of Myer's in the 1930s, told Donald Honig in *Baseball Between* the Lines that Myer was "one of the most rugged competitors I ever saw. Off the field he was the nicest, most placid guy in the world; but the moment he put on his baseball uniform, his personality changed; he became aggressive and pugnacious. It was the most amazing thing; you wouldn't think it was the same person."

Gulfport native Gerald Walker, another outstanding player who bloomed in the 1930s, was considered a character in everything he did, on and off the field. "Though he stole as many as 30 bases in a season, he could be a bungler on the basepaths, inattentive and overzealous. He once tried to steal a base while a batter was being given an intentional walk, and in another game he was caught off base twice in the same inning."

Nicknamed "Gee," the Ole Miss alumnus came up with the Detroit Tigers in 1931, when he shared center field with his brother, Hub Walker, also a Gulfport native. Gee started in center in 1932 and hit .323. He moved to left field in 1933 and batted .280.

In 1934, the Tigers acquired Goose Goslin from Washington, inserted him in left field and created the so-called G-Men contingent — Charlie Gehringer and Hank Greenberg were the other two — that would lead Detroit to the World Series in '34 and '35. Gee Walker became a reserve in those two seasons but had a game-tying hit in the second game of the 1934 Series. True to form, Walker got picked off after that hit, "but the popular Mississippi boy was forgiven," wrote Frederick Lieb in his 1946 team history, The Detroit Tigers.

Walker became a starter again in 1936 and hit .353, and he followed up with a .335 average, 18 homers and 113 RBIs in '37. On opening day of that year, Walker hit for the cycle; no one before or since (through 2011) has turned that trick. "Yet Tiger management, unappreciative of Walker's antics, traded him to the White Sox after the season." He would be traded four more times, finishing his career as a 37-year-old backup with the seventh-place Cincinnati Reds in 1945.

~ ~ ~

Claude Passeau also might fairly be described as colorful. The Waynesboro native, a Millsaps graduate, gained a reputation as a spitballer and was warned on more than one occasion by the commissioner's office that he would be banned if caught throwing the illegal pitch. "I just laughed and told them to have at it," he said in an interview long after his retirement. "I didn't pay any attention to them, 'cause I knew I wasn't cheating. I didn't even know what I was doing myself. That was just my natural fastball."

Passeau had a thing for the number 13, too. He wore it on his uniform—but his devotion went further than that. "That's my lucky number," he once said. "My auto tag is 13. The serial number on my rifle is 13. The last two digits on my life insurance policy are 13 and my address is 113 London Street." By some odd coincidence, it has been noted, "Claude Passeau" is 13 letters long, and he pitched 13 years in the major leagues.

In his prime, the 6-foot-3, 200-pound Passeau was one of the best right-handers in the National League, a four-time All-Star Game selection. In fact, Passeau was a key figure in one of the Midsummer Classic's greatest moments. He threw the pitch that Ted Williams socked for the game-winning home run in the 1941 game at Briggs Stadium in Detroit. The National League led 5-3 in the bottom of the ninth. Passeau was working his third inning in relief for the National League.

The American League loaded the bases with one out. Joe DiMaggio was up, and Passeau got him to hit what looked like a routine double-play grounder to short. But Eddie Miller and second baseman Billy Herman messed up the exchange at second. DiMaggio beat the throw to first as a run crossed.

That brought up Williams, who had struck out against Passeau in his previous at-bat. "Passeau was always tough," Williams said in Robert Creamer's Baseball in 1941. "He had a fast tailing ball he'd jam a left-handed hitter with, right into your fists, and if you weren't quick he'd get it past you. He worked the count to two balls and one strike, then he came in with that sliding fastball around my belt, and I swung."

The ball took off toward right field, and the crowd of 54,674 rose to its feet. The ball "soared on a high arc and hit against the green woodwork at the front of the roof high in right field," Creamer wrote. "Three runs scored. ... Williams, laughing, clapping his hands, leaping like a young colt, bounded his way around the base paths and touched home plate. ... Never before was so much emotion shown by All-Star players after the game. The National Leaguers swore, kicked over their stools, ripped off their uniforms. There was angry second guessing."

Passeau, dazed, had this to say afterward: "I threw him one about chest high. It must have been the wrong thing to do."

Harry Danning, the catcher for the NL team that day, recalled the moment like this in an interview with *Baseball Digest*: "Passeau threw him a slider. We told him not to throw it to Ted, but he did. I went out there three times to tell him to throw his sinking fastball, so he threw the slider and the next thing I knew it hit the top of the stands and the game was over."

Williams, one of the game's all-time greats, always referred to that home run as "the most thrilling hit of my life. It was a wonderful, wonderful day for me."

Passeau's other most notable moment is much more flattering. On Oct. 5, 1945, pitching for the Chicago Cubs in the last war-scarred World Series, he hurled a one-hitter against Detroit in the third game, beating the Tigers 3-0. It was only the second Series one-hitter in history, a dominating performance. For Detroit fans, "it was about as interesting as watching a dear friend being led to the gallows," Lieb wrote. "'When the hell do we start?' more than one Tiger fan yelled during the hitless afternoon. They never did. Only two Detroiters reached base. Rudy York cracked the team's lone hit, a long single to left center with two down in the second inning. The only other Tiger to reach base was catcher (Bob) Swift, who walked in the sixth. ... (T)hough the dose of whitewash was bitter and hard to take, Detroit fans generously applauded the super pitching by the gallant Cub right-hander."

Alas, the Cubs lost that World Series 4 games to 3, and through 2013, they had not been back to the Fall Classic since. Passeau made three appearances in the Series but got only the one decision. He pitched two more years in the majors, both for the Cubs, before retiring in 1947 at age 38. He was 2-6 with a 6.29 ERA that final season, but he did throw one last shutout, the 26th of his career.

More than just an outstanding pitcher, Passeau also fielded his position well. And did so while wearing a small glove because of an injury to his left hand sustained as a kid. Passeau set a major league record for consecutive errorless chances by a pitcher— 273, covering 145 games from September 1941, to May 1946.

~ ~ ~

The 1930s brought change to baseball, some of it a result of The Great Depression, some of it just evolution. The home run was king, but the stolen base was re-popularized by the St. Louis Cardinals' Gas House Gang, which played a hell-bent style that produced five world championships between 1931-46. Relief pitchers began to appear with more frequency in the 1930s, and gloves were improved. The first night game was played in 1935, and a Mississippian participated in it. Radio took on a prominent role in shaping the game's status as the national pastime, with Mississippi native Red Barber spearheading that charge. Barber also broadcast the first televised game in 1939.

The minor leagues were stung by the Depression but recovered handsomely. From a low of 14 leagues in 1933, the minors grew to 44 leagues by 1940. Branch Rickey's farm system, instituted in 1921 to feed players to his St. Louis Cardinals club, became the standard operating procedure for all big league organizations by the mid-1930s.

Cities all over Mississippi fielded minor league clubs in this era. Meridian was represented in the Cotton States League from 1905-08, 1910-13 and 1922-29. The so-called Queen City also had a team in short-lived Mississippi State League in 1921 and in the Southeastern League from 1937-42 and 1946-50.

This rich baseball history might have had something to do with the inordinate number of Meridian-born players who crashed the major leagues in the early part of the 20th century. Between 1915 and 1945, seven players from Meridian suited up for major league clubs. Eric "Boob" McNair and Skeeter Webb were the most prominent members of this group, which also included Joe "Doc" Evans, Danny Clark, Sammy Holbrook, Charlie Moss and Pap Williams.

McNair, whose nickname was taken from the Rube Goldberg comic strip character Boob McNutt, played in 1,251 big league games with four different American League teams. He was a reserve infielder on the champion Philadelphia Athletics teams of 1930 and 1931 and was the starting shortstop for the club in 1932, when he hit 18 home runs. A decent fielder, McNair led

American League shortstops in double plays in 1934—but also led the loop in errors. He finished up with Detroit in 1942, batting .274 for his career. He died seven years later.

Webb, who stood 5 feet 9 and weighed a mere 150 pounds, hung around the majors for 12 seasons and 699 games despite hitting just .219 for his career. He broke in with the St. Louis Cardinals in 1932, resurfaced with Cleveland in 1938 and moved to the Chicago White Sox in 1940. In 1944, a year before he joined the Detroit Tigers, he married the daughter of Tigers manager Steve O'Neill. In 1945, by coincidence, perhaps, Webb was the Tigers' starting shortstop when they played in the World Series and beat Claude Passeau and the Chicago Cubs. Webb's last year in the big leagues was spent with the 1948 Philadelphia A's.

Evans, nicknamed "Doc" during his playing days, actually became a physician after baseball. He played 11 years in the majors and hit .259. Most of his career was spent with the Cleveland Indians, and he was with their World Series-winning team in 1920, the year the Tribe's shortstop, Ray Chapman, was killed by a pitch from the New York Yankees' Carl Mays. Evans, an outfielder and third baseman, batted .349 in 1920 and went 4-for-14 in the Series.

Most of the Mississippians who played in the major leagues between 1920 and 1945 did so in relative obscurity, but some of their tales deserve recounting.

Of Moss Point native Sam "Sambo" Leslie, a left-handed hitting first baseman with a .300-plus career average, it was once written: "He could hit if you woke him up at 2 in the morning but couldn't field if you played him at 2 in the afternoon." Leslie was a pinch-hit specialist and fill-in for most of his career. But in 1936, with the New York Giants, he replaced an injured Bill Terry at first base and helped the Giants win the National League pennant by hitting .295 with 54 RBIs in 117 games. Terry, who was also the Giants' manager, returned to the lineup for the World Series; Leslie went 0-for-3 as they lost to the Yankees.

Starkville's Hughie Critz, a Mississippi A&M (State) graduate, also was a pretty fair hitter. He played 1,478 games over 12 seasons and collected 1,591 hits. But perhaps none of those hits were more memorable than his first two, which came in his big league debut in 1924 against the great Grover Cleveland Alexander. Critz, 5-8, 147 pounds, was the regular second baseman for the 1933 Giants, who, with Carl Hubbell and Mel Ott leading the way, won the world championship.

Ellisville's Harry "Popeye" Craft was better known for his glove and his speed than his bat. In fact, some considered him the finest center fielder of his day, which ran from 1937-42. Fittingly, he caught the final out of the second of Johnny Vander Meer's back-to-back no-hitters in 1938. Craft batted .253 in 566 career games, all with the Cincinnati Reds. He was on their championship teams of 1939 and 1940.

Craft's most noteworthy hitting achievement might have occurred on July 15, 1939, when he belted a ball into the left-field bleachers at the old Polo Grounds in New York off the Giants' Hal Schumacher. Although the ball appeared to be foul by several feet, third-base umpire Ziggy Sears ruled it a home run.

The umpire crew chief, George Magerkurth, confirmed Sears' call and "all hell broke loose," Talmadge Boston wrote in *1939: Baseball's Pivotal Year*. "Giants shortstop Billy Jurges punched Magerkurth, and big George later admitted to league president Ford Frick that the fight was as much his fault as Jurges's. Frick later fined both umpire and player, and suspended them for ten days. Soon after that game, major league parks started putting screens on foul poles to help the umpire's determine whether balls hit into the seats on the line were fair or foul."

The incident may have been a pivotal moment, but "left vague to this day is the logic as to why a ball that hits the foul pole is fair."

Craft became a manager after his playing days and had the good fortune to have Mickey Mantle in the future Hall of Famer's first two pro seasons, with the 1949 Independence, Kansas, team and the 1950 Joplin, Missouri, club. "I was lucky to have Harry as skipper my first two years," Mantle once told the Houston Chronicle. "He started me out right." Craft also managed parts of seven years in the majors, including the 1962 season with the expansion Houston Colt 45s.

Ike Pearson, whose career ERA was 4.84, led all National League relievers with a 2.07 mark as a member of the Philadelphia Phillies in 1941. But many Brookyln Dodgers fans would remember the Grenada native as the pitcher who beaned Pete Reiser that same year. The picture of an unconscious Reiser being carried off Ebbets Field has appeared in many publications over the years. Reiser returned from the injury, after which many Dodgers players began to wear protective headgear.

Like a lot of others in this era, Mississippians lost playing time while serving in the military. Pearson spent three years in the service, as did Hub Walker of Gulfport. Both returned to the field after the war, Walker getting back on the field with the Detroit Tigers, at age 38, after a seven-year absence from the majors. He received a commissioner's waiver to participate in the 1945 World Series against the Cubs and picked up a championship ring.

Columbia's Buddy Blair may have seen his playing career derailed by military duty. As a 32-year-old rookie third baseman, he hit .279 for the 1942 Philadelphia A's. He spent the 1943-45 seasons in the service and never played another major league game.

Atley Donald was a good pitcher who was over-shadowed by bigger stars on some great New York Yankees teams. But the Morton native's niche in baseball lore was secured on October 5, 1941. He was the starter for the Yankees in Game 4 of the World Series against Brooklyn and stood to get the loss before Mickey Owen's infamous passed ball opened the door for the Yanks to win the game and, some say, the entire series.

We can't tell much about Booneville native Glenn Bolton as a major league hitter—but apparently he could run. He managed only two hits in 13 at-bats in four career games with the 1928 Cleveland Indians. Both of the hits were triples.

Jim Bivin of Jackson also played only one season, as a pitcher for the 1935 Phillies, but he had a hand in two significant games. On May 24 of that year, at Cincinnati, Bivin picked up a save in the first night game ever played in the major leagues. The Phillies beat the Reds 2-1. Six days later, back in Philadelphia, Bivin induced Babe Ruth to ground out in the last at-bat of the Babe's incomparable career.

The year 1946 marked the first post-war year for baseball, but, more significantly, it also saw the arrival of the first black player in so-called "organized ball," a euphemism for the white-owned game that had barred blacks since the turn of the century.

Jackie Robinson was that pioneer black player, and three Mississippians helped him blaze a trail that changed the game—yet again.

Spotlight

Gee, What a Day!

One of the rarest feats in baseball is hitting for the cycle, i.e., getting a single, double, triple and home run in one game. Through the 2011 major league season, it had been done 255 times in the game's modern history (since 1901). Only once has it ever been done in the first game of the season. Give it up for Gerald Holmes "Gee" Walker, pride of Gulfport.

The right-handed hitting outfielder accomplished his cycle on April 20, 1937, before a crowd of 38,200 at Navin Field in Detroit. Walker, playing right field for the Tigers and batting fifth (behind Hank Greenberg and ahead of Goose Goslin), homered, tripled, doubled and singled—in that order—in a 4-3 win over Cleveland.

All four hits came against Indians ace Mel Harder, who gave up eight hits and six walks in eight innings that day. Walker belted his home run—one of a career-high 18 he would hit in 1937—in the second inning, putting Detroit ahead 2-1. He tripled and scored in the fourth inning as the Tigers rallied for two runs to go ahead 4-3. Elden Auker, Detroit's starter, shut the Indians down from there. Walker, a career .294 hitter, batted .335 that season, his seventh in the majors. He finished his 15-year career with 1,991 hits: 1,392 singles, 399 doubles, 76 triples and 124 homers, one of each on April 20, 1937.

Truly One of a Kind

An Arkansan by birth, Dizzy Dean adopted Mississippi as his home, and the Magnolia State returned the favor by embracing as its own the man who was a Hall of Fame pitcher, an award-winning broadcaster and a genuine all-around character.

Born Jay Hanna Dean—or Jerome Herman Dean, as he sometimes claimed—in Lucas, Arkansas, in 1911, he married a Mississippi woman named Patricia Nash and settled in Bond, in south Mississippi, after he retired from baseball.

Shortly after Dean's death in 1974—he was buried in Bond — a museum was built in Jackson in Dean's honor, and per his wish, a treasure trove of his baseball memorabilia went on display there. In 1991, Dean was inducted into the Mississippi Sports Hall of Fame. The Dean museum was incorporated into the Mississippi Sports Hall of Fame and Museum, a state-of-the-art facility that opened in Jackson in 1996.

Beginning in 1950, Dean brought national attention to Mississippi virtually every week during the baseball season as the colorful and sometimes controversial color commentator for the CBS Game of the Week, a job he held for over 20 years. He introduced the nation to words like "slud" (meaning slide), swang (swung) and throwed (threw). Dean had a down-home sense of humor that perhaps only Southerners could fully appreciate. Once, on the Game of the Week, play-by-play announcer Pee Wee Reese boasted about catching a catfish more than a foot long. "We got 'em down in Mississippi like that, too," Dean shot back, "but that's between the eyes."

Dean's major league playing career, which began in 1930 with the St. Louis Cardinals, was brief but profound in its impact. Among the numerous testimonials he has received over the years are these:

• "Dizzy Dean's career has been likened to the dramatic suddenness, glow and abrupt disappearance of a comet." (Ritter and Honig, *The Image of Their Greatness*.)

• "In the Depression years, Dean was just the man to represent baseball. ... His folksy, no-nonsense ways made a lot of sense to a confused and frightened generation." (Johnson, *Baseball's Dream Teams*.)

• "(F)or six years, he was brilliant. He gave baseball a unique spark, and drove (Cardinals owner) Branch Rickey to distraction in the process. 'If there was one more like him,' Rickey said, 'I'd get out of the game.'" (Kerrane, *The Hurlers*.)

• "His popularity and colorful approach to the game continued unabated when he entered the radio broadcasters' booth. His malapropisms and blatant avoidance of the rules of grammar were legendary, and fans loved it." (*The Ballplayers*.)

Dean, given the nickname Dizzy while pitching and befuddling hitters in the service, is famous for coining the phrase "It ain't braggin' if you can do it," and he could pretty much do anything with a baseball. He once shut out the Boston Braves throwing nothing but fastballs, which he had announced he would do before the game began.

The tall right-hander averaged 24 wins a year for his first five full seasons (1932-36) in the big leagues, all with the Cardinals. He led the National League in strikeouts four times and whiffed 17 in a game in 1933.

Dean was 30-7 for the 1934 World Series championship club, called the "Gas House Gang" for its grungy look and gritty style. Led by Frankie Frisch, Leo Durocher, Rip Collins, Joe Medwick and Pepper Martin, the Cardinals beat Detroit in seven games in 1934. Dean was 2-1 in the Series, throwing a shutout in Game 7. His brother, Paul, won the other two games for the Cardinals.

It was in the 1937 All-Star Game at Griffith Stadium in Washington that Dean's brilliance was dimmed. A line drive off the bat of Cleveland's Earl Averill hit Dean on the toe. When a doctor told Dean the toe was fractured, Dean reputedly said, "Fractured, hell, the damn thing's broke." Dean tried to come back too soon, altered his pitching motion and injured his arm. He slumped to 13-10 that season. Traded to the Chicago Cubs in 1938, he went 7-1 with a 1.80 ERA for a pennant-winning team. He pitched sparingly for the Cubs over the next three seasons, never able to revive his arm or recapture his magic.

In 1947, six years after retiring from the game, Dean was working as a broadcaster for the lowly St. Louis Browns when, on a dare, he took the mound again. At age 36, he tossed four scoreless innings.

Dean was elected to the National Baseball Hall of Fame in 1953. He died on July 17, 1974, and an all-star list of dignitaries came to Mississippi for the funeral. Among the thousand or so mourners were Hank Aaron and Ducky Medwick, a teammate of Dean's from the "Gas House Gang" days.

Dean was buried near a magnolia tree in the middle of the Bond cemetery. At the close of the service, Medwick famously said, "Well, that's the ballgame."

The Voice of the Game

He never threw a pitch or swung a bat in a professional baseball game. But Walter Lanier "Red" Barber, the son of a railroad man from north Mississippi, was one of the true stars of his day. He has a plaque in the broadcasters' wing at the National Baseball Hall of Fame in Cooperstown, N.Y., to prove it.

Barber, a deeply religious and eloquent Southern gentleman, worked 32 years as a major league radio broadcaster, starting with the Cincinnati Reds in 1934 and finishing with the New York Yankees in 1966. But he made his mark in Brooklyn as the smart, composed voice of the Dodgers from 1939-53.

"The three of them, (Larry MacPhail, (Leo) Durocher and Barber, revolutionized baseball in 1939, and Barber's part in the revolution was by no means the least important. ... After Barber and the Dodgers exploded into prominence, baseball broadcasting became as integral a part of a major league club's operation as the third base dugout," wrote Robert Creamer in *Rhubarb in the Catbird Seat*, a Barber biography.

Barber was born in Columbus in 1904. His father, seeking greener pastures in hard times, moved the family to Florida when Walter was about 10. Barber grew up and was educated there (at the University of Florida) before embarking on an exhaustive search for a job in big-city broadcasting in 1934. Despite his relative inexperience—he had worked only at college station WRUF in Gainesville, Florida—he was hired by the Cincinnati Reds. "I broadcast the first major league baseball game I ever saw," he once said.

Barber developed a close relationship with MacPhail, then the Reds' general manager. When MacPhail took a job with the Dodgers in 1938—and subsequently introduced baseball radio broadcasts to New York, where they'd been banned by mutual agreement of the city's three big league teams since 1932—Barber jumped at the chance to join him the next year.

The timing could not have been more perfect. The Dodgers had not been to the World Series since 1920. In fact, they'd been there only twice in their history and lost both times. While their crosstown rivals, the

Yankees and Giants, prospered, the Dodgers became "Dem Bums" to their loyal but long-suffering fans. That began to change with the arrival of MacPhail and Durocher, the brash manager who made famous the line, "Nice guys finish last."

Brooklyn finished first in the National League in 1941, Durocher's fourth year.

"Led by the acid-tongued Leo Durocher, the Dodgers literally fought their way through a season of beanball wars, brawls and umpire baiting to edge out a spirited Cardinal team by 2 ½ games (in the National League pennant race). With Larry MacPhail running the front office and spending prodigal sums of money for players, the moribund, bankrupt Brooklyn franchise had been turned into one of the most exciting in baseball," wrote Lawrence Ritter and Donald Honig in *The Image of Their Greatness.*

Barber was there to spread the news. He even did play-by-play for the first televised baseball game, on Aug. 26, 1939, from Ebbets Field.

"Lord those years were exciting," Creamer wrote. "Everybody talked baseball. If a million people went to Ebbets Field to see the Dodgers play, ten million listened to Red broadcast their games. ... In the summer of 1941 you did not need to own a radio to hear Red broadcast. You could walk up a street and hear the game through one open window after another and never miss a pitch. You could thread your way through the crowd on a beach and get the game from a dozen different portables. In traffic, you'd hear it from a hundred different cars."

The Dodgers, led by the likes of Gil Hodges, Pee Wee Reese, Jackie Robinson, Billy Cox and Roy Campanella, ended their 20-year pennant drought in 1941 and won again in 1947, 1949, 1952 and 1953. Yet when Brooklyn won its first World Series title in 1955, Barber was no longer doing the games; he and the club had parted ways over a contract dispute after the 1953 season. Barber was calling games for the Yankees in '55, when they lost to the Dodgers in the Fall Classic.

The Yankees unceremoniously fired Barber at the end of the 1966 season, claiming he had lost his enthusiasm for the broadcasts. It was reported that Barber blew a kiss toward Ebbets Field—which had been torn down in 1958—after his last game with the Yankees. "I didn't broadcast with a Brooklyn accent," he once said, "but I broadcast with a Brooklyn heart."

Barber did a National Public Radio show for 12 years, a labor of love thoughtfully chronicled by Bob Edwards in the book *Fridays with Red*.

Barber also played a prominent role in the Ken Burns PBS documentary *Baseball*, shedding light in particular on Jackie Robinson's breaking of the major league color barrier in 1947. Barber, a Southerner to the core, wrestled internally with that issue before accepting it, and his even-handed broadcasts no doubt helped Dodgers fans do the same.

Barber had a truly unique way of calling a game. "The first element in Barber's style was that he regarded himself as a broadcaster, not a fan. ... The second feature to Barber's technique involved constantly using his expanded vocabulary and Southern metaphors which came to be known as Barberisms," Boston wrote in *1939: Baseball's Pivotal Year*.

"Whether live from the ballpark or via tickertape, the 'Ole Redhead' as he was called, offered the most literate, appealing account of a baseball game ever heard on the air," wrote Stanley Cohen in *Dodgers: The First 100 Years*. "Not given to theatrics and occasional hysteria that marked the work of other broadcasters,

Barber gave his report of the game in soft understated phrases peppered with colloquialisms all his own."

Said Vin Scully, a Barber protégé who was still doing Dodgers games in 2011, in the Ken Burns documentary: "No one ever came up with the expressions that Red Barber had. What he brought was the country flavor. He became part of the language ... ducks on the pond ... sitting in the tall cotton ... I mean, there were just a million of them. You would suddenly say, 'I wonder what that looks like when somebody leaps up against the wall, or dives into second, or bowls over the catcher ...'"

It was only fitting that Barber and ex-Yankees radio voice Mel Allen were the first broadcasters inducted into baseball's Hall of Fame in 1978.

"Barber's impact on New York was extraordinary," Creamer wrote in *Rhubarb*. "Everybody knew who Red Barber was, even my maiden aunt—literally. The language he used in his broadcasts became part of everyone's speech. ... Much of it sounds dated now— sittin' in the catbird seat, tearin' up the pea patch, walkin' in the tall cotton, we got a rhubarb growin' in the infield, the bases are FOB: full of Brooklyns—but a cliché is essentially a phrase that is so good everybody

77

keeps repeating it. And Barber was good. Mixed in with all the Southern corn were felicitous phrases like 'advancing to third on the concomitant error,' which flattered his ever-more knowledgeable audience, an audience that was ever more knowledgeable primarily because of him.

"He created fans. They learned about the game of baseball just by listening to the old redhead sitting in his catbird seat tearing up the pea patch … He told you about the game. He told you about it fairly and accurately, and he interpreted it, and in doing so he set standards of excellence that have never been surpassed, and seldom, if ever, equaled."

Barber died on Oct. 22, 1992, in Tallahassee, Florida. His sister, Virginia Wynne, said at the time of his death that he still considered Mississippi "home."

Chapter 3

A New Beginning
1946-1960

**Starkville native James "Cool Papa" Bell
was a Negro Leagues star who was
inducted into National Baseball Hall of Fame in 1974
(Courtesy of the Negro Leagues Baseball Museum)**

Lending a Helping Hand

Few athletes have truly transcended their sport.

Jackie Robinson is one of them.

Robinson hit .311 in an 11-year career with the Brooklyn Dodgers, smacked 137 home runs, stole 197 bases and played in six All-Star Games and six World Series.

But in his case, statistics are almost irrelevant.

"The most historically significant baseball player ever, Jackie Robinson was the first black man to play in the majors in the 20th century, to win the MVP award, to be elected to the Hall of Fame (in 1962); was also the first Rookie of the Year and the first baseball player, black or white, on an American postage stamp. Babe Ruth changed baseball; Jackie Robinson changed America."

Three Mississippians played important, if behind-the-scenes, roles in Robinson's passage into history.

Starkville native James "Cool Papa" Bell, a Hall of Fame outfielder in his own right, helped prepare Robinson on the field for what awaited him in the major leagues. Greenwood's Clay Hopper was Robinson's first manager in so-called "organized baseball," with the minor league Montreal Royals in 1946. And Columbus native Red Barber, the longtime radio voice of the Brooklyn Dodgers, broadcast Robinson's rookie season in the majors, an experience that would prompt Barber to write a book titled: *The Year All Hell Broke Loose in Baseball.*

Branch Rickey, who became president and general manager of the Brooklyn Dodgers in 1942, had made up his mind to break the gentlemen's agreement that had kept blacks out of the major leagues since the turn of the 20th century. For several years, he looked for the right man for his "great experiment." He found him in Jack Roosevelt Robinson, a young Negro Leagues player from Cairo, Georgia, who had been a four-sport star at University of California at Los Angeles and was an Army veteran.

"When Kansas City Monarch Jackie Robinson first met Branch Rickey in August of 1945, all the Negro Leaguers immediately knew that Robinson might be chosen to integrate the game. This filled them with great anxiety because Robinson was a rookie in the Negro league, relatively inexperienced. Quickly, the old-time baseball men pulled together in an effort to teach Robinson the trade in as short a time as possible. Playing for the Homestead Grays in the twilight of his career,

Cool Papa Bell was approached by Dizzy Dismukes of the Monarchs, who informed Bell that Robinson was on the verge of signing with the Dodger organization. 'He wants to play shortstop,' Dismukes told Bell, but Dismukes and everybody else on the Monarchs knew that Robinson would not be able to play major-league shortstop. Bell's concern was strong. 'If he missed his chance, I didn't know how long we'd go before we'd get another,' he recalled in Donn Rogosin's *Invisible Men*.

"Dismukes requested Bell to hit into the hole and test Robinson's move to the right, and he asked Bell to give Robinson a base-stealing exhibition because the Negro leaguers were not impressed with Robinson's tagging ability. Bell, who 'ran like he stole something,' easily beat out two infield hits that went to Robinson's right, and he stole four bases that night. Coming into second just under Robinson's tag, he said, 'See that? They got a lot of guys in the major leagues who slide like that. You can't get those guys out like that.'"

Ultimately, Bell and other Negro League veterans convinced Robinson that second base or the outfield might be a better position for him. "'One night I must have knocked a couple hundred ground balls to his right, and I beat the throw to first every time,' Bell said in a

Sports Illustrated story by Mark Kram. 'Jackie smiled. He got the message. He played a lot of games in the majors, only one of 'em at short.'"

On Oct. 23, 1945, Robinson signed to play with the Dodgers' Class AAA Montreal affiliate. Two weeks later, Rickey selected Mississippi native Hopper to manage the Montreal club. The reaction was predictable. From Jules Tygiel's *Baseball's Great Experiment*: "'Hopper is a gent with a drawl from the deep South and he is going to have to handle Jackie Robinson,' noted Canadian sports writer Baz O'Meara. 'Oh! Oh!' commented the Baltimore Afro-American."

Hopper, a Mississippi A&M (now Mississippi State) graduate and a cotton farmer in the off-season, was a career minor leaguer who spent 32 years playing or managing in the bushes. He had been a protégé of Rickey's and a manager since 1929.

"Two frequently cited quotations illustrate Hopper's alleged distaste for his new assignment," Tygiel wrote. "The Mississippian, it is said, pleaded with Rickey to send Robinson elsewhere. 'Please don't do this to me,' he reputedly told Rickey. 'I'm white and I've lived in Mississippi all my life. If you're going to do this, you're going to force me to move my family and home out of Mississippi.' On a later occasion, when Rickey described a Robinson catch as 'a superhuman play,' Hopper reportedly responded, 'Mr. Rickey, do you really think a nigger's a human being?'

"These stories may be true, but Rickey, who had so carefully orchestrated the integration scenario, had not rashly cast Hopper in this critical role. ... (Rickey) hoped Hopper's Mississippi origins might mute dissension and serve as an example of a white southerner willing to accept blacks on his team."

Indeed, to his everlasting credit, Hopper did accept the job; he wasn't forced into it. "He agreed to manage the Royals after the Dodgers had publicized their integration venture," Tygiel noted. But opinions differ on the nature of the relationship between Hopper and Robinson during that season in Montreal.

Rachel Robinson, Jackie's wife, would say years later in Art Rust Jr.'s *Get That Nigger off the Field*:

"Jackie's first manager at Montreal, Clay Hopper, never really believed in this but was just doing as he was told. I thought he saw Jackie as a commodity. He just evaluated Jackie as somebody who could help him win, somebody who drew crowds, somebody who could spark up the games, and most of all, somebody who Mr.

Rickey was intent on holding. Therefore, it was Hopper's job to make it work. In other words, Hopper knew he was stuck with Jackie. Hopper never went out of his way to be friendly. As he chewed on his tobacco, he said Jackie was doing his job. Hopper was a Mississippian. He played Jackie only as much as he had to play him. At the end of the season, Clay appeared to come around to a certain extent, but you never could distinguish between whether he was feeling that Jackie was more of a human and he had learned something in this experiment or whether he was just happy to have a winning ballclub."

Broadcaster Red Barber, on the other hand, claimed that Hopper and Robinson worked well together. "(T)he relationship between Hopper and Robinson was splendid," he told writer Robert Creamer. "Jackie told me so. Jackie was surprised, he said, but pleased. He found that Hopper was a fair man. When you get around to life, isn't that all it's supposed to be? Be a fair man?"

Montreal, with Robinson leading the league in hitting, won the International League pennant in 1946. The city rejoiced. From Geoffrey Ward and Ken Burns' *Baseball: An Illustrated History*: "Clay Hopper, the Montreal manager who had questioned Robinson's humanity before the season started, now clasped Robinson's hand: 'You're a great ballplayer and a fine gentleman,' he said. 'It's been wonderful having you on the team.'"

Barber had a much more difficult time with the Robinson situation than did Hopper. Rickey told Barber in 1944, a full year before Robinson was signed, that a black player would be joining the Dodgers soon. Barber wondered why Rickey would tell him this in confidence.

"I gave him back 100 percent silence, because he had shaken me. He had shaken me to my heels. And I think that is why he told me, because he knew it would shake me. He always told me that I was the most valuable person in Brooklyn to him and the ballclub," Barber told Creamer.

Barber was born and raised a Southerner. By all accounts, he was a fair and honest man and deeply religious. He had grown up around black people, called many his friends; he was hardly a venom-spewing racist. "But there was a line drawn, and that line was always there," he told Creamer.

Rickey's news forced Barber to come to grips with those deep-seated prejudices. His initial reaction was to quit his job. His wife counseled patience. Barber tried, as

Creamer reported: "… The thing was gnawing at me. It tortured me. I finally found myself doing something I had never really done before. I set out to a deep self-examination. I attempted to find out who I was. This did not come easily, and it was not done lightly."

Barber reflected on the pure accident of birth that made him white and placed him in Mississippi. He also turned to his religious faith. While preparing for a radio talk on the issue of race that he had been asked to do by a clergyman, Barber found some answers he could live with. "… I remembered something about Bill Klem, the great umpire," he told Creamer. "Klem always said, 'All there is to umpiring is umpiring the ball.' … I took that and worked over it a little bit, and I said, 'Well, isn't that what I'm supposed to do? Just broadcast the ball? Certainly a broadcaster is concerned with who is at the plate—you're deeply concerned. … But still, basically, primarily, beyond everything else, you broadcast the ball —what is happening to it. All you have to do is tell the people what is going on."

When Robinson made his major league debut on April 15, 1947, Barber was ready for the momentous occasion. "Jackie Robinson's coming to the Dodgers didn't bother me at all," he would write. "By the time

Jackie was selected by Rickey … I had found personal peace."

Robinson was sensational that first season despite the vicious heckling he took from opposing fans and players. Huge crowds came to see him, at home and on the road. Playing first base, he batted .297, led the league in stolen bases with 29, scored 125 runs in 154 games and won the first Rookie of the Year Award. He also helped the Dodgers win the NL pennant; they lost the World Series to the Yankees in seven games.

Barber, nothing if not modest, took little credit for helping Robinson make it through that difficult season: "If I did do anything constructive in the Robinson situation, it was simply in accepting him the way I did — as a man, as a ballplayer," he told Creamer. "I didn't resent him, and I didn't crusade for him. I broadcast the ball."

Both Robinson and Rickey expressed to Barber that they felt he did it the right way, thereby helping rather than hindering baseball's great experiment. Yet Barber felt like he was the one who was helped. As he put it in Creamer's book, "Well, what I am trying to say is, if there is any thanks involved, any appreciation, I thank

Jackie Robinson. He did far more for me than I did for him."

Twinkles in the Galaxy

Baseball took another quantum leap in 1946. Just as Babe Ruth's power and personality had altered the game in 1920, so did Jackie Robinson's in 1946, when he became the first black player in so-called "organized baseball" in the 20th century, opening the door for others.

World War II was over, and all of the major league stars were back on the field by the 1946 season. Post-war prosperity brought other changes to the game, not all of them positive. Still, for most Mississippians in the big leagues, these were good times.

The high-water mark for Mississippi's influence on the national pastime might have come on Oct. 15, 1946, in St. Louis' old Sportsman's Park. Game 7 of the World Series featured a Mississippi boy on the mound for the American League champions and another native son in left field for the National League champs.

David Meadow "Boo" Ferriss, the starting pitcher for the Boston Red Sox that day, was a tall right-hander from Shaw, up in the Delta.

Harry William "The Hat" Walker, from the Gulf Coast town of Pascagoula, was a left-handed hitting outfielder for the St. Louis Cardinals.

Their big league careers intersected that fall for the first and only time. In Game 7, Ferriss was knocked out of the box by the Cardinals in the fifth inning, having allowed three runs. The Red Sox came back to tie.

In the eighth, with Enos Slaughter on first base and two outs, Walker ripped a pitch from Bob Klinger into the gap in left-center field. Slaughter, in one of baseball's immortalized moments, dashed all the way home, scoring just ahead of the throw by startled shortstop Johnny Pesky. The Cardinals held in the ninth and won the championship. Baseball was back in a big way.

~ ~ ~

Ferriss was 25 in 1946, in just his second season with the Red Sox after his military hitch. Walker was 28 and just back from three years of war duty. He first came up with the Cardinals in 1940, a product of Branch Rickey's expansive farm system.

91

Ferriss was an eye-popping 25-6 with a 3.25 ERA in 1946. This followed a rookie season in which he was 21-10 and beat every team in the American League the first time he faced them. Led by Ferriss and the hitting of the great Ted Williams, the Red Sox ran away from Detroit to win the American League pennant, beating the Tigers by 12 games. Williams batted .342 with 38 homers.

In the 1946 National League race, the Cardinals and Brooklyn Dodgers tied for first place. St. Louis swept a best-of-3 playoff to claim the pennant. Walker was the starting left fielder most of that season, though he played in only 112 games, hitting .327 with three homers and 27 RBIs. The Cardinals' big bat was Stan "The Man" Musial, who had a phenomenal year with a .356 average, 16 homers, 103 RBIs, 20 triples and 50 doubles.

While the Cardinals and Dodgers were playing off for the National League title, the Red Sox were sitting around, waiting to learn their destination for the World Series opener. "We were all packed to go, but we had that delay while the playoff was going on," Ferriss said years later. "Having to wait like that, I think it took the edge off us. We played some all-star teams to try to stay sharp, but it wasn't the same. And Ted Williams got hit on the elbow that week, though he never used that as an excuse in the Series."

The 1946 World Series, as it turned out, was one of the best ever, rich with dramatic moments even though Williams managed just five singles in the seven games. The Red Sox won the opener in St. Louis 3-2 in 10 innings. St. Louis came back in Game 2 with a 3-0 win on Harry "The Cat" Brecheen's four-hitter.

Ferriss took center stage in Game 3 at Boston's Fenway Park, scattering six hits and walking just one in a 4-0 victory. Rudy York's three –run homer in the first inning off the Cardinals' Murray Dickson was all the support Ferriss would need. "Of course, they still had eight innings to play, but Ferriss was in pinpoint form, and answered Brecheen's earlier shutout with one of his own," wrote Timothy Baker Shutt in a piece for *Sports History* magazine. "At the end … Ferriss had raised his winning streak at Fenway to an incredible 14 games."

Back came the Cardinals in Game 4, pounding out 20 hits off six Boston pitchers on their way to 12-3 win. Harry Walker was 1-for-2 with an RBI, his first of the Series, for St. Louis. The games were now even at two apiece. Boston took Game 5 6-3 behind a four-hitter by Joe Dobson. Walker drove in all three Cardinals runs.

The teams returned to St. Louis, where, in Game 6, Brecheen tossed a seven-hitter to beat the Red Sox 4-1. The seesaw Series was headed to a Game 7.

Oct. 15, 1946, was the same day 11 Nazis were sentenced to hang for crimes against humanity in World War II. At Sportsman's Park in St. Louis, baseball was doing its small part in helping America's recovery. Ferriss started for the Red Sox against Dickson, the same matchup as in Game 3. Game 7 was filled with dramatic moments. Boston scored in the top of the first on a sacrifice fly by Dom DiMaggio, but St. Louis answered with a sac fly by Walker in the second. It was still tied 1-1 going to the St. Louis fifth, when the Cardinals surged ahead.

"It was pure pandemonium when Dickson finally got his revenge on Ferriss," Shutt wrote. "With leftfielder Harry Walker on second, the little pitcher crushed a double down the left-field line, scoring Walker. Red Schoendienst joined in the festivities with a single to center that drove in Dickson. When Terry Moore also singled, Ferriss was pulled for Joe Dobson."

DiMaggio's two-out double in the eighth off St. Louis reliever Brecheen—coming back the day after throwing nine innings in Game 6—drove in two runs for Boston and knotted the score again at 3-3.

Bottom eighth: Slaughter led off with a single against Bob Klinger. After a popped-up bunt and a lazy fly, Slaughter was still at first base with two down.

Then along came Harry Walker. From *Baseball's Unforgettable Games*: "Slaughter, like a thoroughbred at the barrier, was itching to be off. Eddie Dyer, the St. Louis manager, leaned out of the first base coaching box and gave Slaughter the sign to take off with the pitch. If Walker missed the pitch, it would stand as an attempted steal. If he connected, the hit and run would be on. The breaks were riding with the Cards. Walker drove a low, screaming liner into safe territory in left center."

Slaughter ripped around second base, tore into third and kept going. He scored easily with what would prove to be the winning run. Walker had his sixth and easily biggest RBI of the Series. Brecheen would blank the Red Sox in the ninth, giving St. Louis its sixth world championship.

"Slaughter had speed—and smarts. Regular Red Sox center fielder Dom DiMaggio had injured his ankle on the basepaths after driving in the tying runs with two outs in the eighth. His replacement, Leon Culberson,

95

didn't have DiMaggio's arm, and everybody — including Slaughter—knew it," wrote Paul Adomites in *October's Game*.

~ ~ ~

The home run was still considered the key to offense in the 1950s. The slider became an effective new weapon for pitchers during this period, but in 1950 the strike zone was altered, squeezing the plate for pitchers.

"(T)he scale was beginning to tip in favor of the pitchers — not through rule changes, but through the convergence of trends: night games, specialized relief pitching, proliferation of the slider, and evolution of stadium architecture," according to Kevin Kerrane in *The Hurlers*. With the aid of the smaller strike zone, hitters would continue to rule until 1963, when the zone was enlarged.

Off the field, greater changes took place in the 1950s as the post-war high began to subside. It wasn't as bad as the Depression Era, but baseball again experienced money troubles. From Charles C. Alexander's *Our Game*: "Baseball's financial woes related to major changes in where and how Americans lived. The economic boom of the post-World War II years enabled millions of families to leave the cities and relocate in suburbs, where they developed distinctly suburban life-styles, largely independent of what was happening in the city—at least as far as entertainment and recreation were concerned. Meanwhile, the areas around the ballparks tended to decay and become crime-ridden, a particularly discouraging circumstance in light of estimates that about forty percent of baseball customers were now women and children."

Television also had a negative impact on attendance, particularly in the minor leagues, as it kept fans in their homes. As owners sought greener pastures, the first franchise shifts occurred in the 1950s, the Boston Braves moving to Milwaukee in 1953, the St. Louis Browns to Baltimore (as the Orioles) in 1954, the Philadelphia A's to Kansas City in 1955 and, of greatest significance, the Brooklyn Dodgers to Los Angeles and the New York Giants to San Francisco in 1958.

Players had attempted to organize a guild in the late 1940s, forcing owners to make concessions on minimum salaries and pensions. The Mexican League lured some players away from the U.S. with big money offers in the mid-'40s, though most were back in the States within a couple of years.

Yet if these were tough times for some in the game, they were good for others, particularly black players who were, at long last, getting opportunities to play in the major leagues. After Jackie Robinson famously broke the color line in 1947, it took only two years for a Mississippian to reach the majors: Jonestown native Luke Easter made it with the Cleveland Indians in 1949. Easter was followed by Crawford's Sam Hairston with the Chicago White Sox in 1951, Potts Camp native Bob Boyd with the White Sox that same year, Dave Hoskins of Greenwood with the Indians in 1953, Frank Barnes of Longwood with the St. Louis Cardinals in 1957 and Jackson's Marshall Bridges with the Cardinals in 1959.

All first played in the Negro Leagues, the black man's alternative to the majors, and arrived in The Show at a relatively late stage of their career. They were the pioneers for the Magnolia State.

Easter was 34 when he made it to the big leagues. He played in 491 games, all with the Indians, from 1949-54 and hit .274 with 340 RBIs. Known for his power, he belted 28 homers in 1950 and 31 the next year. He played Triple-A ball well into his 40s but never made it back to the majors after being released in 1954.

Hairston appeared in just four games with the White Sox in his only season in the big leagues. He went 2-for-5 as a 31-year-old rookie. He recalled his first at-bat in The Show: "It was Comiskey Park (in Chicago), off Connie Marrero (of the Washington Senators). I got a hit. In fact, I drove in the only run we scored that day." Hairston's sons Jerry and John and grandsons Jerry Jr. and Scott also played in the majors, making them the first black three-generation big league family.

Nicknamed "The Rope" for the line drives he hit to all fields, Boyd played five seasons in the Negro Leagues and was 25 when he was first called to the majors by the White Sox in 1951. He was 30 when he finally became a regular, in 1956 with Baltimore. A first baseman, Boyd batted .311 that season, in which he was limited to 70 games by an elbow injury. He hit .318 in 1957 and .309 in '58 and ended his major league career in 1961 with a .393 average over 693 games.

Hoskins was a standout hitter and pitcher in the Negro Leagues and became the first black to play in the Texas League before joining the Cleveland Indians in 1953 at the age of 28. "The Indians management had some difficulty deciding which role he should play in their organization, as an outfielder or pitcher," according to James A. Riley's *The Biographical Encyclopedia of the Negro Leagues*). Cleveland used him primarily as a pitcher. In his two years in the big leagues (1953-54), Hoskins, a right-hander, was 9-4 with a 3.79 ERA, and he owns the distinction of having surrendered the first home run of Al Kaline's Hall of Fame career. Hoskins hit .227 with a homer in limited batting opportunities.

The first black Mississippian to play in the National League, Barnes was acquired by St. Louis in 1957 and was 29 when he made his debut. The right-hander pitched in 15 games over three seasons, posting a 1-3 record and a 5.84 ERA. He pitched a number of years in the Mexican League after leaving the majors. He apparently harbored some resentment about his limited time in The Show. "I can't even watch baseball on TV," he told *The Clarion-Ledger*. "All of that money and I'm not getting anything. I played like 22 or 23 years of professional baseball, no lower than Triple-A for 12 years or more."

Bridges, a left-hander called "The Sheriff," pitched in 206 big league games, breaking in with the Cardinals two years after Barnes did. Bridges went 23-15 with a 3.75 ERA. He had the good fortune to play with the New York Yankees in 1962-63, during the Mickey Mantle era. In fact, Bridges, like most newcomers to the club, was subjected to a rite of passage with the Yankees in 1962 that involved Mantle. Former Yankees second baseman Bobby Richardson: "Mantle was the main jokester. We had a pitcher—Marshall Bridges—who was deathly afraid of snakes. Mantle bought a fake snake, put it in an ice box, tipped everyone off and then put it in Bridges' pants leg," wrote Stan Olson in Baseball Digest. That tale was repeated many times in the days surrounding Mantle's death from cancer on Aug. 13, 1995.

~ ~ ~

The brightest stars from Mississippi during the period from 1946-60 were clearly Boo Ferriss and Harry Walker, who met in that classic World Series in 1946.

Ferriss, after a brilliant rookie year in 1945, had one of the best seasons ever by a Mississippi-born hurler in '46, winning 25 games and looking for all the world like he'd be a Boston ace for years to come. But his career began a downward spiral after the '46 Series. He went 12-11 with a 4.04 ERA in 1947 and 7-3 with a 5.23 in '48, when he pitched mostly in relief. A shoulder injury and asthma problems drove him from the game by 1950. His career numbers are still impressive: 65-30, 3.64 ERA in 144 games. He would return to Mississippi and establish himself as a truly legendary coach at Delta State in Cleveland, near his home of Shaw.

Walker's career included one more major highlight after the '46 Series. In 1947, after being traded during the season from St. Louis to the Philadelphia Phillies, he won the NL batting crown with a .363 average. He would play parts of six more seasons in the big leagues, including a brief comeback in 1955 as a player-manager after four years off the field. He went 5-for-14 at age 38 that season. Walker took his nickname "The Hat" from his habit of tugging on his cap between every pitch of his at-bats and allegedly went through 20 hats a season. It worked for him: He batted .296 in an 807-game career spent with four different teams.

Walker managed parts of nine seasons in the big leagues, with St. Louis, Houston and Pittsburgh. He never won a pennant, but his career record was a commendable 630-604 (.511 winning percentage). He also served as a big league hitting coach and was with the Cardinals when they won the 1964 World Series. Like Ferriss, he went on to coach college baseball, at the University of Alabama-Birmingham, and their teams faced each other many times.

A number of other capable if lesser known Mississippians broke in during this period, chief among them Don Blasingame, a Corinth native who played 1,444 big league games with five teams over 12 seasons. Primarily a second baseman, Blasingame batted a respectable .258 for his career and made the National League All-Star team in 1958 with St. Louis, the club he came up with. Blasingame, who swung from the left side, could hit to all fields, bunted well and ran exceptionally well. He grounded into a double play just once every 123 at-bats, one of the best ratios of all-time. His speed also accounts for the two nicknames he picked up: "Blazer" and "The Corinth Comet." Blasingame also had a knack for breaking up no-hit bids in late innings, which he did four times in his career.

Like several other Mississippians in the majors, Blasingame also is remembered for his link to a much bigger star. In 1963, Cincinnati Reds manager Fred Hutchinson benched Blasingame, "one of the Reds' most popular players ... and installed a raw rookie named Pete Rose at second base," Dave Anderson wrote in *Pennant Races*. Rose, who would go on to become baseball's all-time hit king, batted .273 that season. Blasingame played only 18 games for the Reds that year before he was traded to Washington, a last-place club in the American League. He played regularly for the Senators for three seasons, was traded to the Kansas City Athletics in 1966 and retired that year at age 34. He later played, coached and managed in Japan.

Wilmer Mizell was a left-handed pitcher from Leakesville who was better known by his nickname, "Vinegar Bend," which derived from an Alabama town in which Mizell once played ball. He went 90-88 with a 3.85 ERA over nine seasons in the majors. He had a tendency to be wild—he led the league in walks in his rookie year of 1952 with the Cardinals — but was a real battler on the mound, described in *The Ballplayers* as "consistent but unspectacular." Mizell once threw a four-hit shutout that included nine walks. He made the National League All-Star team in 1959 and went 13-5 for the world champion Pittsburgh Pirates in 1960. Mizell entered politics after his playing career ended and served a lengthy stint as a U.S. congressman from North Carolina.

West Point's Bubba Phillips, a former football and baseball star at Mississippi Southern College (now Southern Miss), was another solid player who arrived in the big leagues in the 1950s. A third baseman most of his career, Phillips played in 1,062 games with three clubs and batted .255. His peak season might have been with Cleveland in 1961, when he led American League third baseman in homers with 18. He batted .264 with 40 RBIs for the 1959 pennant-winning Chicago White Sox, a light-hitting team known as the "Go-Go Sox."

Injuries sidetracked the career of Mississippi City native Milt Bolling, an infielder who hit .241 in 400 games from 1952-58. Dave Madison, from Brooksville, had an 8-7 record and a 5.70 ERA in 74 games from 1950-53. Vaughn native Hugh Laurin Pepper pitched in 44 games for Pittsburgh in the mid-'50s, and Benton's Fred Waters posted a 2.89 ERA in 25 games with the Pirates during the same time. All told, 19 Mississippians appeared in the majors from 1946-60. A new and much larger wave would follow in the new and very different era that dawned in 1961.

The 1960s mean many things to Americans: Vietnam, the assassination of President Kennedy, the hippie movement, racial turbulence, the invasion of The Beatles, the space race. In baseball, the 1960s meant, among other things, expansion, for the first time in the 20th century. A Mississippi native managed the first major league team to play in Houston, and another

105

Magnolia Stater played for New York's new team, the Mets, who in 1962 played some of the worst baseball ever witnessed.

The 1960s was a dynamic decade, and it was only the beginning of what was becoming a whole new ballgame.

Too Little, Too Late

Though he was a good-natured man, kind to strangers and children and well-respected by his peers, Luke Easter's life was framed by tragedy.

Easter, from the Delta community of Jonestown, died in a tragic manner. On March 29, 1979, in Cleveland, Ohio, he was shot and killed by two robbers, who made off with the $45,000 Easter was carrying in a shopping bag. As the chief steward for an aircraft workers union, Easter often handled large sums of cash, and one of the robbers apparently knew him.

Easter's major league career also was tinged with sadness. When the roll is called for the great sluggers in baseball history—Babe Ruth, Mickey Mantle, Hank Aaron, Willie Mays, Reggie Jackson, Mark McGwire, Barry Bonds, et. Al—Easter's name isn't likely to come up. After all, he hit just 93 home runs in the big leagues.

The tragedy is that his name probably would be mentioned in the same breath with the other great sluggers had times been different. Easter began his pro career in the Negro Leagues, debuting with the Homestead Grays in 1947. By the time he was signed by the American League's Cleveland Indians—becoming the first black Mississippian to make the majors—he was 34 and past his playing prime. He had lied about his age to enhance his chances of getting into the majors; the Indians believed him to be 28.

His big league career lasted just six seasons, all of 491 games.

To be sure, Easter accomplished some noteworthy things in his short tenure with the Indians. A tall, left-handed hitting first baseman, he blasted 28 homers in 1950, 27 in 1951 and 31 in 1952 as Cleveland began to make serious challenges to the New York Yankees' dynasty. But Easter was cursed by injuries. He played in just 68 games in 1953 and by the fall of 1954, when the Indians charged past the Yankees and made the World Series, Easter was back in the minors. He never returned to The Show.

"Most of all, Easter represents a generation of black players robbed of that right to be remembered," noted

Daniel Cattau in *Smithsonian Magazine*. Case in point: As of 2011, Easter was not in the Mississippi Sports Hall of Fame.

Throughout his playing days, Easter was believed to have been born in 1921 in St. Louis, where he grew up. But later research by Cattau revealed that Luscious Easter actually was born in 1915 in Jonestown. His family grew cotton there until 1924, when, shortly after the death of Luke's mother, Easter's father sold the land and moved the family to St. Louis.

Easter played semipro ball in St. Louis as a kid and later, after a hitch in the military, caught on with a black touring club called the Cincinnati Crescents. The Homestead Grays, a Negro Leagues powerhouse, were looking for a successor to their late slugger Josh Gibson when they spotted and signed Easter in 1947.

Easter stood 6 feet 4 and weighed 240 pounds and was blessed with incredible power as a batter. "I hit 'em and forget 'em," he once said. All told, he hit 385 lifetime homers, including Negro League, major league and minor league games.

"He also had a reputation for fearsome skills as a gambler. A card shark, he loved playing cards and engaged in the pastime at every opportunity, often using a marked deck. Although he was fun-loving, friendly and charismatic, his dishonest tendencies with a deck of cards often caused him trouble," according to James A. Riley's *The Biographical Encyclopedia of the Negro Leagues*.

Bill Veeck of the Cleveland Indians signed Easter to a major league contract in 1949, and he quickly established himself as a long-ball threat with few if any equals. "Everywhere he played, he left behind stories of his gargantuan home runs," Riley wrote.

During a Negro League game in 1948, Easter blasted a 475-foot homer to center field at New York's Polo Grounds, the place where Willie Mays made his iconic over-the-shoulder catch in the 1954 World Series. Easter's homer is believed to be the only ball ever hit out of that park to center field. "He hit it halfway up the stands, about 500 feet," teammate Bob Thurman claimed in Cattau's magazine piece. "Thing about it—it was a line drive."

In 1950, the Indians "thought so highly of the left-handed hitter that they traded Mickey Vernon, a once and future American League batting champ, making Easter their everyday first baseman. He hit 28 home runs as a rookie; one, a 477-foot shot, is considered the longest ever hit at Cleveland Municipal Stadium," according to *The Ballplayers.*

Easter also hit a tape-measure homer for the minor league Buffalo Bisons that has become the stuff of legend.

"On July 14, 1957, Luscious Luke did something no one had ever done—he hit a ball so high and so far that it sailed over the (Offermann Stadium) center-field scoreboard, 400 feet away," Lawrence Ritter wrote in Lost Ballparks. "Including the advertising signs atop it, the scoreboard was 60 feet high! On August 15 of the same year, he almost repeated the feat — this time the ball cleared the 42-foot high scoreboard but hit one of the advertising signs on top of it."

Broadcaster Frank Messer remembered another Easter home run, also coming at Offermann Stadium, as the longest he had ever seen: "Luke hit the ball over the right field fence, over the street and over a row of houses on the fly. It hit the roof of a house in the next row and fell into the backyard. I had never seen a ball hit like that in my life." When Messer told Easter where the ball had landed, Easter asked him if he were sure. "I saw it all the way," Messer told *Baseball Digest.* "If you saw it all the way," Easter replied, "then it wasn't the longest home run ol' Luke ever hit."

"Maybe there is such a thing as 'the natural,'" said Al Rosen, a former teammate of Easter's.

Consider that Easter was in his 40s when he led the Triple-A International League in home runs and RBIs in 1956 and 1957, and he finished near the top again in those categories in 1958. He was "an immediate folk hero in Buffalo, as he had been previously in Cleveland, due as much to his charismatic personality as to his long-distance batting feats," Ritter wrote.

Easter continued to play minor league ball until 1964, retiring at the age of 48. He was 63 when he was killed. Some 4,000 fans attended his wake in Cleveland and another thousand were at the funeral. The city of Cleveland honored the slugger posthumously by naming a park after him and erecting a bronze bust of his likeness on the grounds there. A plaque reads: "Strong, courageous and beloved as a baseball player and as a man." Sadly enough, relatively few people, particularly in his home state of Mississippi, know much about Easter as a player or a person.

Spotlight
All Things Considered

At the top of the list for major league victories by a Mississippi native is Guy Bush, who won 176 games, 14 more than Claude Passeau and 22 more than Roy Oswalt, who was still pitching in 2011. Further down the list —but worthy of mention—is Boo Ferriss, who won 65 games before injuries curtailed his promising career. William Foster isn't on the list at all. Baseball's color barrier kept the Rodney native out of the major leagues. But the left-hander won a lot of games in a lot of other leagues during a long career that, in 1996, earned Foster a plaque in the National Baseball Hall of Fame.

According to baseball-reference.com, Foster won 128 games in various Negro Leagues, including 72 in a five-year span from 1926-30. "Willie Foster's greatness was that he had this terrific speed and a great, fast-breaking curve ball and a drop ball, and he was really a master of the change of pace," former teammate and manager Dave Malarcher said in *Only the Ball Was White*, Robert Peterson's fascinating book about black baseball. "He would throw you a real fast one and then use the same motion and bring it up a little slower, and then a little slower yet. ... He was really a great pitcher." One performance that might serve as testament to this greatness came in the summer of 1933 at old Comiskey Park in Chicago.

The occasion was the first East-West All-Star Game, an exhibition that would become the showcase event for the Negro Leagues. Foster, then with the Chicago American Giants, pitched the West to an 11-7 victory.

Here's the impressive part: He worked all nine innings and limited to seven hits a lineup that reads like a Who's Who of Negro Leagues stars: Cool Papa Bell, Rap Dixon, Oscar Charleston, Biz Mackey, Josh Gibson, Jud Wilson, Judy Johnson, Dick Lundy and Vic Harris among them. Though he never won a major league game, the case could be made that William Foster was the best pitcher Mississippi ever produced.

There Were Others

The anecdotes, some of them just tall tales, that have been attached to the playing career of Starkville native James "Cool Papa" Bell ensure that he will never be forgotten by those who track baseball history.

Here's a sampler:

• Bell was once hit in the back by his own batted ball as he slid into second base.

• Bell once scored from first base on a bunt, and he also stole two bases on one pitch.

• "If he bunts and it bounces twice, put it in your pocket," Double Duty Radcliffe, a former teammate of Bell's from the Negro Leagues, once claimed.

• It was said that Bell could turn out the lights and jump into bed before the room got dark. The great Satchel Paige used to tell that one.

Fact or fanciful elaboration, those stories attest to Bell's greatest natural gift, his legs, which literally and figuratively carried him a long way. Though he never played a game in the major leagues, he "rode the crest of the publicity from his incredible speed and colorful nickname into the Hall of Fame," James A. Riley wrote *in The Biographical Encyclopedia of the Negro Leagues.*

Elected to Cooperstown by the Veterans Committee in 1974, Bell also was belatedly inducted into the Mississippi Sports Hall of Fame in 1994, three years after his death. The entrance road to the Jackson-based Sports Hall of Fame and Museum and Smith-Wills Stadium, the venerable ballpark, was named Cool Papa Bell Drive, also in 1994.

Bell was a slightly built man (5 feet 11, 150 pounds) who played some 28 years in the Negro Leagues and Latin America during the time—pre-Jackie Robinson — when blacks were effectively banned from the major leagues.

"Power is stark, power shocks, it is the stuff of immortality, but Papa's jewellike skills were the object of shoptalk for 28 winters," Mark Kram wrote in *Sports Illustrated.* "During (Bell's) career he had been the essence of black baseball, which has a panache all its own. It was an intimate game; the extra base, the drag bunt; a game of daring instinct, rather than one from the hidebound book. Some might say it lacked discipline, but if so, it can also be said that never has baseball been played more artfully, or more joyously."

For sure few have played it more artfully than Bell.

From Robert Peterson's *Only The Ball Was White:* "In 1945, when he was forty years old, he was still one of the base-stealing leaders of the Negro national League. Bell played such shallow center field that occasionally he was able to sneak in behind a runner at second base and trap him while the first- and third-base coaches were watching the infielders. His arm was mediocre, but he overcame this weakness by getting rid of the ball quickly."

Bill Veeck, whose career as a general manager in the major leagues spanned several eras, once said Bell was "the equal (defensively) of Tris Speaker, Joe DiMaggio or Willie Mays. Another baseball man compared him with Wee Willie Keeler as a hitter and Ty Cobb as a base runner," wrote Stephen Hanks.

Bell left Starkville at the age of 16 and moved to St. Louis, where he was noticed playing company baseball and signed by the St. Louis Stars, an established Negro League club, at the age of 22. A pitcher originally, Bell moved to center field after hurting his arm. He consistently batted in the high .300s and stole bases at an amazing clip.

He got the ☐ickname "Cool Papa" from Stars manager Bill Gatewood, a nod to Bell's poise under pressure. From 1922-38, Bell played on three of the best and most storied teams in Negro Leagues history: the Stars, the Pittsburgh Crawfords and the Homestead Grays. He also toured with the famed Kansas City Monarchs in the latter stages of his career.

"Bell was a selfless player and fans recognized and appreciated this quality in his character," Riley wrote. "Cool Papa's popularity was evident—he was voted to the East-West All-Star Game every year from its inception in 1933 through 1944, except for the five years he was playing in Latin America."

Mississippian William Foster, a star left-handed pitcher on some great Negro Leagues clubs of the 1920s and 1930s, was elected to the National Baseball Hall of Fame in 1996, 18 years after his death. Foster played on three championship teams with the Chicago American Giants and was the winning pitcher in black baseball's first East-West All-Star Game in 1933. Originally listed as having been born in Texas, Foster is now acknowledged to be a Rodney native. He attended Alcorn State and later served as the Dean of Men at the Lorman college.

As members of the Hall of Fame, Bell and Foster are the exceptions among black players from the early

20th century. So many stars of the old Negro Leagues will never receive the recognition they are due, and among this group are quite a few Mississippi natives. Take, as a prime example of this injustice, Howard Easterling, born in Mount Olive in 1911.

The day after Easterling died, on Sept. 6, 1993, in Collins, a five-paragraph obituary appeared in *The Clarion-Ledger*. It referred to Easterling as a "retired baseball player" and a military veteran. The brief obit mentions that Easterling played in the Negro Leagues and for an all-star team organized by Satchel Paige. No report on Easterling's death appeared in the paper's sports section. It wasn't an oversight. It's just that no one knew of his significance in the game.

Easterling was a five-time All-Star during his 12 years in the Negro Leagues, playing from 1936-49, with two years off for his military duty. A switch-hitting third baseman, Easterling could "run, throw, field and hit with power," Riley wrote.

In his five appearances in the East-West All-Star Game—the true showcase event for Negro Leaguers— Easterling batted .320. He began his career with the Cincinnati Tigers before being recruited to play for the powerful Homestead Grays in 1940. With Easterling and future Hall of Famers Josh Gibson and Buck Leonard in the middle of their batting order, the Grays won four straight Negro National League pennants and the Negro League World Series title in 1943. After serving in the war, Easterling played three more years in the Negro Leagues and then finished his career in Mexico in 1953.

Despite his obvious talents, Easterling never received a tryout from a major league club. He was 36 when Robinson broke the color line in 1947, still a capable player. It is worth noting that Easterling almost beat Robinson into so-called organized baseball. In 1943, Clarence "Pants" Rowland, the president of the Class AAA Pacific Coast League's Los Angeles Angels, announced that he was going to give tryouts to three Negro Leaguers, Easterling, Chet Brewer and Nate Moreland. But Rowland decided against the move two weeks later, "apparently under pressure from other league operators," according to Peterson.

During the heyday of the Negro Leagues — from the 1920s into the mid-1940s—some games were played in Mississippi, according to Buck O'Neill, the iconic black baseball spokesman from the Ken Burns' documentary series. In fact, Satchel Paige reportedly was discovered by a Negro League team from Chattanooga while playing in a semipro game in Gulfport in the '20s. But no Negro League teams made their home in Mississippi.

The list of Mississippi-born players who appeared in Negro League games before 1950—when black-only baseball pretty much faded away—includes Luke Easter, Sam Hairston, Bob Boyd, Dave Hoskins, Marshall Bridges and Frank Barnes, all of whom got to the major leagues, plus a number of others who didn't get that opportunity.

Crawford native Hairston, whose grandsons Jerry Jr. and Scott were playing in the majors in 2011, was a Negro Leagues standout who got only five at-bats with the Chicago White Sox in 1951. Primarily a catcher, Hairston won the Negro American League Triple Crown in 1950 with a .424 average, 17 home runs and 71 RBIs in a 70-game season. He has been described as a "rough-and-tumble player."

Other Mississippians who made a mark with outstanding Negro League teams include David "Lefty" Harvey of Clarksdale, who played for the Pittsburgh Crawfords in 1935; Rufus Lewis of Hattiesburg, a pitcher with the 1946 Newark Eagles; Alfred "Buddy" Armour, a Jackson native who played for the Cleveland

Buckeyes in 1945; and Sherwood Brewer, from Clarksdale, a pitcher for the 1948 Kansas City Monarchs.

Research in Riley's Negro Leagues encyclopedia also turns up Lovell "Big Pitch" Harden from Bay St. Louis, Jackson's William Black, Hattiesburg's Henry McCall, Meridian-born Lacey Thomas, Buddy Hoskin of Canton, Bill Hoskins of Charleston, Albert "A.D." Clark from Fayette and Bubba Hyde from Pontotoc.

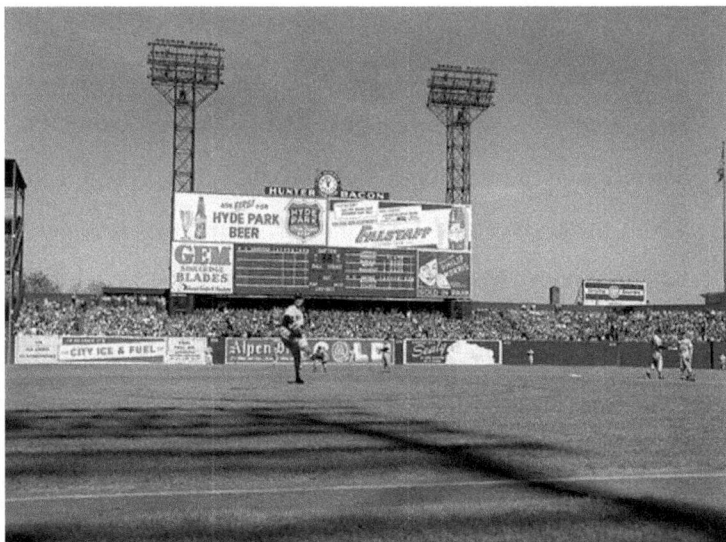

Sportsman's Park, site of the 1946 World Series

Hyde, sometimes called "Bubber," enjoyed a long career as an outfielder in black baseball, breaking in with the Memphis Red Sox in 1927 and hanging on until 1951 with various clubs. He got his first tryout with the Memphis Red Sox at the age of 14.

Some claim that Hyde was almost as fast as Cool Papa Bell. "Cool Papa may have had Bubba by a smidgen," Verdell Mathis, a former teammate of Hyde's with Memphis, told *The Clarion-Ledger*. "They were both so fast you couldn't hardly throw them out if they hit the ball on the ground."

Hyde claimed to have no regrets that he didn't get a shot at the major leagues. He was 39 when baseball was integrated. "We were treated well," he later recalled. "I had enough money, and I loved the game. You can watch these days and you can tell some guys play just for the money. Most of us played because we loved it. I have no regrets. I had a nice time— a real nice time— and I loved every minute of it."

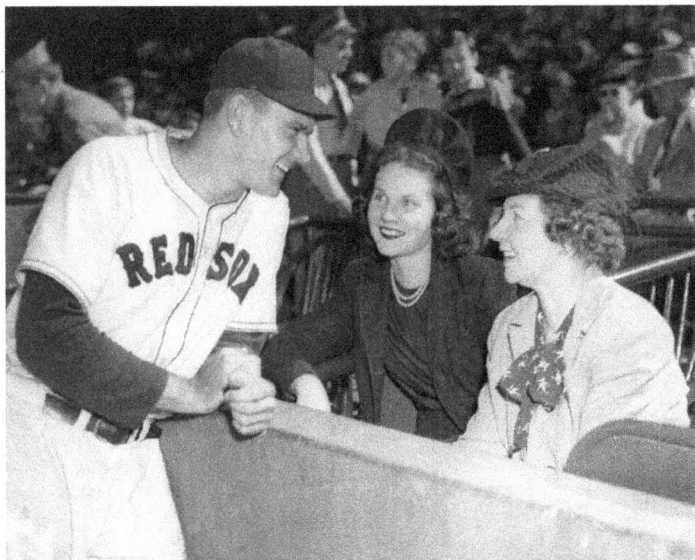

**Dave "Boo" Ferriss, with sister Martha Anne
and mother Lellie
Courtesy Mississippi Sports Hall of Fame and Museum**

Chapter 4

Twinkles in the Galaxy
1961-1994

George "Boomer" Scott hit 271 home runs during
14-year career
Courtesy Mississippi Sports Hall of Fame and Museum

Dreams Do Come True

It was called "The Impossible Dream," taking its name from the hit song in the Broadway musical *Man of la Mancha*. The Boston Red Sox, who finished ninth in the 10-team American League in 1966, rose up to win the pennant in 1967, captivating the city and much of New England if not the entire country.

"Never has a pennant race been closer than the American League's of 1967, and never has there been a more improbable winner or a more heroic star," wrote William B. Mead in *The Explosive Sixties.*

That winner, Boston, a 100-to-1 longshot at the start of the season, earned its first World Series trip since 1946. The heroic star was Carl Yastrzemski, a New York native and the Red Sox left fielder, who won the Triple Crown by leading the league in batting average, home runs and RBIs.

The 1967 season was also a dream come true for Greenville native George Scott. He wasn't the hero that Yaz was to the burgeoning Red Sox Nation, but the man they called "Boomer" was a major contributor. He hit .303 that year, fourth-best in the AL, and added 19 homers and 82 RBIs.

Scott overcame some long odds to get there. He came from the dirt-poor Delta, a child of the deeply segregated 1950s and 1960s. "His father had died when he was an infant, and his mother worked a succession of menial jobs trying to keep food on the table for Scott, his brother and sister," Bill Reynolds reported in *Lost Summer*, a book about the 1967 Red Sox. "The family lived in a tarpaper shack. ... He didn't grow up rebelling against the existing social order. He didn't grow up militant. He just wanted to play ball. His mother, Magnolia, always taught him to work hard, be respectful of people, and good things would happen."

Scott became a star athlete at Greenville's Coleman High School, excelling in football, basketball and baseball. Many college recruiters came calling, and major league scouts also found their way to the Delta.

\ Seven of them showed up at Coleman on the night Scott graduated. He accepted a signing bonus from the Red Sox of $10,000 — "more money than he knew existed in the world. ... George Scott knew nothing about the Red Sox or their racial history. He had no idea where Boston was, or anything about it. He bought some land for his mother and a used black-and-yellow GTO for himself," Reynolds wrote.

Boston was the last major league club to integrate, bringing up Pumpsie Green in 1959, 12 years after Jackie Robinson's debut with the Brooklyn Dodgers. Scott arrived in Boston in 1966. The team was lousy, but Scott was a success. He blasted 27 homers, drove in 90 runs and made the American League All-Star team as a 22-year-old rookie first baseman.

Scott would enjoy a nice career in the majors, one practically devoid of controversy. He played in three All-Star Games. From *The Ballplayers*: "Likable and colorful George Scott, with his well-spaced gold teeth and sometimes bulging waistline, was a fan favorite in Boston. A flashy fielder, he collected eight Gold Gloves, a record for first basemen."

He could swing the bat, too, hitting .268 with 271 homers and 1,051 RBIs in his career, most of it spent with the Red Sox. Yastrzemski once said Scott was a threat to break Roger Maris' 1961 record of 61 homers. He never approached that figure, but in 1975, while with Milwaukee, he tied for the American League lead with 35 homers and led the loop with 105 RBIs. He returned to Boston in 1977 and hit 33 homers, but he faded after that and was out of the big leagues by early 1979.

If he had one problem, it was his weight. In 1965, when he won the Double-A Eastern League's Triple Crown, Scott played at 198 pounds. Two years later, during "The Impossible Dream" season, he was up to 220. Near the end of his career, he was listed at as much as 240. Fiery Dick Williams, Boston's rookie manager in 1967, made an issue of Scott's weight during spring training of that season. Scott, an upbeat sort, never seemed to let it bother him. He just kept plugging away, as did all of the Red Sox in that remarkable season, and he will always have a place in Red Sox lore.

"Let me explain something," Scott told *Sports Illustrated* when he was playing in Mexico in 1981. "I was born poor, I was born black, and I was born in Mississippi. When you've been through that, you can deal with anything. The only thing I was ever taught was survival. The name of the game for me is survival."

Two other Mississippians figured in the great pennant chase of 1967, which involved four teams and went down to the season's final day. McComb native Dalton Jones was a teammate of Scott's in Boston and hit .289 as a spare infielder. Clarksdale's Fred Valentine was with the Washington Senators, and he got a key hit in a late-season game that eliminated the Chicago White Sox from the race.

On Sept. 18, 1967, with about two weeks left in the season, only a half-game separated the four contenders for the American League crown: the Red Sox, the White Sox, Detroit and Minnesota. Ten days later, with three days left, all four still had a shot.

Chicago dropped out first. On the next-to-last day of the season, Boston beat the Twins twice to eliminate them and clinch a tie. With Yaz leading the way, the Red Sox won again the next day, October 1, and the race came down to the second game of a doubleheader between California and the Tigers. As the Red Sox listened on the radio in their clubhouse, the Angels won the game, eliminating Detroit.

Boston headed to the World Series for the first time in 21 years. Alas, the Red Sox lost the Series in a thrilling seven games to St. Louis and the great pitcher Bob Gibson. Scott batted just .231 but had four of Boston's 14 hits against Gibson, who beat them three times. The defeat didn't diminish "The Impossible Dream" for Scott. Only days after the World Series ended, Greenville held a parade for him.

Years later, on a visit to Fenway Park with Reynolds, Scott looked around wistfully and said, "'Baseball is huge around here now. But without us (the 1967 team), it wouldn't be the same.' Amen, Boomer, Amen."

Red Sox fans, as passionate as any in any sport, would suffer seven-game World Series losses again in 1975 and 1986. The so-called "Curse of the Bambino," reputedly placed on the franchise when owner Harry Frazee sold Babe Ruth to the New York Yankees after the 1919 season, finally lifted in 2004, when the Red Sox won their first world championship since 1918. They would win another crown in 2007.

Twinkles in the Galaxy

This period in baseball was marked by fundamental alterations in the game both on and off the field, and it came to a stunning and gloomy end. New teams were added to both leagues in several rounds of expansion, and there were more franchise shifts. The designated hitter was born. Free agency helped fuel the emergence of the celebrity superstar who sold his services to the highest bidder.

Whether any of the many Mississippi-born players of this era grew to true superstar status is debatable, but several did enjoy outstanding careers.

Hitting and pitching grab most of the attention in baseball, and players with the skills to hit long home runs or throw 95 mph pitches command the most money, too. But baseball is much more than bombs and strikeouts. Defense is critically important, as well. No championship team has ever been weak in that phase of the game.

"Defense is baseball's visible poetry and its invisible virtue," wrote Thomas Boswell in *Why Time Begins on Opening Day.* "Defense is also the vital, but easily torn, web of order that runs through the game, giving a team a sense of itself as more than a motley of individuals. Above all, fine defense is the often ignored common denominator of champions … We forget that an American child's first baseball pleasure is catching a ball. Hitting comes later, pitching last. First, we learn that magic of plucking a speeding object out of the air; eventually, we do it with a graceful certainty. Throw a child a ball and watch his look of amazement the first time he stabs his arm in the air and actually discovers the ball has lodged in his glove."

One of the Mississippi's best-ever players was best known for his work with the glove. Frank White, a Greenville native who emerged on the big league scene in the 1970s, didn't hit quite enough to capture the fancy of Hall of Fame voters, but his defense would have to be regarded as Cooperstown quality.

White played 19 years, all for the Kansas City Royals, and won eight Gold Gloves at second base, including six in a row from 1977-82. In 1988, at age 38, he committed just four errors in 150 games. "You're unbelievable. I've never seen anything like it," said Bill Buckner, a longtime big leaguer and a teammate of White's in 1988.

White wasn't a bad hitter by any means. He batted .255 with 886 RBIs for his career. When the Royals won the American League pennant in 1980, White hit .264 with 60 RBIs and nine stolen bases. In 1985, when the George Brett- and Bret Saberhagen-led Royals won the World Series, White frequently hit cleanup, slugging a career-high 22 homers and driving in 69 runs.

Still, defense was his legacy. As David Falkner wrote in *The Sporting News* in 1995: "White was an innovator, a gambler as well as a ballet artist. In the course of playing, he developed a unique flip, one that players today still cannot—or will not dare to—emulate. The side flip most infielders use is from close range, within 10 feet or so of the bag. White, by coordinating the flip with a tricky little jab step forward, was able to get much more on the throw and from greater distances. ... Another innovation was his way of coming to the bag to receive a shortstop's throw. Instead of going directly to the base, White circled slightly to the back of it and then seemed to glide forward so that when he took the ball he would be in a continuous, flowing motion going into his pivot and throw."

White, born in Mississippi in 1950, moved to Kansas City as a kid and grew up there. He was signed by the Royals out of a tryout camp and attended the club's baseball academy, becoming in 1973 the first graduate of that unique baseball finishing school to make it to the big leagues.

He is a legend in Kansas City, which retired his number 20—picked to honor playing great Frank Robinson—during the 1995 season.

That defense is a somewhat overlooked phase of the game always troubled White. "If you look at every team in baseball, and if there is a guy who can hit but can't play defense, that guy is still going to play," White told *Street & Smith's* magazine. Not being a big home run hitter is "going to hurt a lot of guys like myself in the Hall of Fame voting," he said, "because everybody is judged by Babe Ruth. An infielder's got to have a different judging system."

~ ~ ~

The allure of the power hitter is what gave rise, in 1973, to the designated hitter rule in the American League. Many designated hitters never took the field. Many AL clubs started carrying more pitchers, some of whom would face only one batter in a given appearance. The closer, the ninth-inning reliever, became commonplace in both leagues. And yet, in this era of specialization, Mississippi produced an impressive number of players who could shine with bat and glove.

George Scott, another Greenville native, was known as "Boomer" for his powerful bat. But he also hit for average—.268 career with two .300 seasons—and he was outstanding in the field, winning eight gold gloves, a record for first basemen. A big man, he was still graceful enough to play third base early in his career and handled the hot corner very well.

Jackson native Chet Lemon, a center fielder who played 16 years in the majors, set American League records for chances (524) and putouts (512) in 1977 for the Chicago White Sox. Lemon's "hustling, aggressive style of play became his trademark," according to *The*

Ballplayers. He could hit, too, batting .273 with 215 home runs and adding 58 stolen bases.

Lemon was traded from Chicago to Detroit in 1982 and was joined in the Tigers' outfield that season by Larry Herndon, a Sunflower native who could also run and catch. Herndon had been named the National League rookie of the year in 1976 when he played center field for the San Francisco Giants. The Tigers put Lemon, Herndon and Kirk Gibson—all capable of playing center—in the same outfield, and this defensive strength was a key to Detroit's championship run in 1984. Like Lemon, Herndon could handle the bat. He hit .273 for his career.

Calhoun City native Dave Parker may be one of the most talented athletes Mississippi has ever produced. He hit 339 career homers, won two batting titles (in 1977 and 1978) and an RBI crown (in 1985). He also turned heads with his defense, particularly his throwing arm. Parker replaced the great Roberto Clemente in right field in Pittsburgh in 1973 and went on to win three Gold Gloves at that position. His powerful right arm was said to compare with that of Clemente and was best shown off during the 1979 All-Star Game, when Parker cut down two runners on the bases.

Parker was huge—listed at 6 feet 5, 230 pounds during his 1978 NL MVP season—but fluid in the field. He had an eye-popping 27 assists during the '77 season.

In 1979, the year the Willie Stargell-led Pirates won the World Series over Baltimore, Pittsburgh manager Chuck Tanner said of Parker in a *Street & Smith's* story, "Dave will be an even greater player when he is between 30 and 35 years old. The reason is simple enough. Parker is intelligent and he will never stop improving. If he has three great years in a row, he won't look back. He will look ahead. He will say to himself: 'I've got to do something to top last season.'"

Alas, Parker, who was 27 in 1979, had only one more truly great season after that one. Knee problems and weight problems began to drag his career down, and he was also involved in the drug scandal that rocked the Pirates in the early 1980s. Unproductive but carrying a relatively high salary, he "became a villain in Pittsburgh, the target of boos, thrown objects and threats," according to *The Ballplayers*.

The Pirates traded Parker to Cincinnati in 1984, and he knocked in 125 runs for the Reds in 1985. But he had become a defensive liability and was shipped to the American League in 1988, and he finished out his career as a designated hitter. He played a part in Oakland's drive to the World Series in 1988 and 1989.

For all his decorations, Parker likely was never as good as he could have been. He slipped off the Hall of Fame ballot after the 2011 voting, essentially ending his chances of enshrinement. Bill James, the noted baseball analyst, put Parker's career in perspective in 1984: "(I)f I had a ballclub, just about everybody would have a weight clause. Why? If you were managing the Pirates over the last three years (1981-83), wouldn't you have wished to God that Dave Parker had a weight clause in his contract?"

~ ~ ~

Expansion of the major leagues—the Los Angeles Angels and Washington Senators (replacing the original Senators who had moved to Minnesota) joined the American League in 1961, the New York Mets and Houston Colt .45s the NL in 1962—thinned out the talent but also opened the door for a rush of new players.

The stolen base as a weapon was taken to new heights by the likes of Maury Wills (104 steals in 1962), Lou Brock (118 in 1974) and Rickey Henderson (130 in 1982). The strike zone was expanded in 1963, in part as a response to Roger Maris' record-breaking 61 homers in 1961, and pitchers regained the advantage they had lost in the 1950s.

"Batting averages during the high strike 1960s are lower than for any decade. The new strike zone made life miserable for hitters," noted Lloyd Johnson in *Baseball's Dream Teams*. After the so-called Year of the Pitcher in 1968, when Bob Gibson posted a jaw-dropping 1.12 ERA, the mound was lowered in 1969.

The 1970s witnessed the first organized player strike (1972), the birth of free agency (1975-76) and wildly escalating salaries, the introduction of the designated hitter in the American League and other types of specialization, including a full-time pinch runner, who just happened to be a Mississippian. The 1980s saw another player strike (1981), a drug scandal and a gambling scandal.

Baseball expanded again in 1969, 1977 and 1993. There had been 16 teams in 1960; by 1993, there were 28. Divisions were created within the leagues, and the postseason was expanded. More franchises moved. New stadiums went up. Ticket prices rose. The World Series became a prime-time television event. Players, who once worked regular jobs in the off-season, were distanced from the fans by their fat contracts; they became stars more than heroes. Some became villains. Kids began to collect baseball cards for their monetary value more than for fun and games.

In a nutshell, baseball became more of a business during this period, never to go back. Money was the thing, a realization brought home like a thunderclap by the disastrous labor dispute of 1994, which resulted in the cancellation of the World Series. It took a while, but the game recovered, as it always has.

This eloquent summation was written by Geoffrey Ward and Ken Burns in *Baseball: An Illustrated History in 1994*: "Everything has changed then; and nothing has changed. Baseball remains a nineteenth century game about to enter the twenty-first century, altered but intact, and still the national pastime. Despite its troubles and the country's; despite Astroturf and television; despite the ignominious departure of Pete Rose and the second coming of George Steinbrenner, the game can still summon up sublime moments of grace and skill and accomplishment that speak to us in our time precisely as they would have spoken to our fathers and grandfathers and great-grandfathers in their time, and as they will delight our sons and daughters in theirs."

The Angels and Senators were the first of baseball's new teams, but the New York Mets stole their thunder a year later. The Mets joined the National League in 1962 and proceeded to post the majors' worst record (40-120) since the infamous Cleveland Spiders of 1899. Yet people, particularly those in the borough of Queens, embraced the Mets.

"The worse the Mets played, the better New York fans, deprived for four years of their beloved Giants and Dodgers, seemed to like them," wrote Ward and Burns. "They lost 17 in a row, 11 in a row, 13 in a row. It didn't matter. Huge crowds came out to chant, 'Let's go Mets! Let's go Mets! No matter what was happening on the field."

Left-handed pitcher Wilmer "Vinegar Bend" Mizell, a Leakesville native, wound up with the 1962 Mets in the last year of what had been an excellent career. Mizell was 90-88 with a 3.85 ERA for his career, spent mostly with the St. Louis Cardinals and Pittsburgh. But at age 31, he was traded by the Pirates to the Mets, for whom he contributed an 0-2 record and a 7.34 ERA. He fit right in with a staff that posted an ERA of 5.04, easily the worst in the majors.

The National League's other new team in 1962, the Houston Colt .45s, also had a Mississippi connection. The Colts were managed by Ellisville native Harry Craft, who guided them to a 64-96 finish, not good but much better than the Mets. Craft, who had been a fine outfielder in his playing days, was 360-485 as a manager with a succession of weak teams. He was also a member of the Chicago Cubs' ill-conceived and ill-fated College of Coaches.

In 1961, Cubs owner Phillip K. Wrigley got the idea to rotate coaches throughout the major and minor league system rather than have one manager assigned at each level. "The idea was to encourage and develop minor league talent as quickly as possible," wrote William B. Mead in *The Explosive Sixties*.

Craft was one of the four head coaches who ran the Cubs that season. His record was 7-9; the Cubs went 64-90 overall—poor but actually better than their 1960 record. Wrigley tried the College of Coaches method again in 1962 and 1963 with similarly bad results. Bob Kennedy, a head coach in 1963, became the manager in 1964 when the project was abandoned.

Another significant event of the 1960s was the collapse of the New York Yankees, who had dominated the game for over 40 years, ever since the Babe Ruth trade of 1920. The Yankees started the decade strongly, winning the World Series in 1961 and 1962.

Silver City's Jack Reed delivered his only career home run for the Yankees on June 24, 1962, to win a game against Detroit in the 22nd inning. Another Mississippian, Marshall Bridges, played a much more prominent role for the Yanks that season.

Jackson native Bridges, a product of the Negro Leagues, went 8-4 with 18 saves for New York in 1962. In Game 4 of the World Series that year, Bridges gave up a grand slam to San Francisco's Chuck Hiller that broke a 2-2 tie in the eighth inning. The Giants won the game to even the series at 2-all. Bridges pitched a scoreless inning in Game 6, which the Yankees also lost before wrapping up the championship in a dramatic seventh game.

Bridges, nicknamed "The Sheriff," allegedly was shot in barroom fight after the 1962 season and was ineffective the following year. He lost the closer's job to Hal Reniff and got into just 23 games, going 2-0 with one save. That was Bridges' last year in pinstripes.

The Yankees lost the World Series in 1963 and 1964, fell to the depths of the American League in 1965 and wouldn't win another pennant until 1976, a stunning drought. From Charles C. Alexander's *Our Game*: "As had happened to all baseball dynasties sooner or later, the Yankees fell victim to age, infirmity, and a lack of sufficient new blood. The extraordinarily productive farm system George Weiss had created—23 clubs and some 600 players in 1949—had dwindled to seven clubs and about 150 players by the mid-sixties. (Mickey) Mantle, the heart of the Yankees for more than a decade, was simply no longer capable of holding up for a full season (because of various leg injuries)."

Unfortunately for Jake Gibbs, a Grenada native and two-sport All-American at Ole Miss, the decline of the Yankees coincided with his ascent to the big leagues. The Yankees had given Gibbs a $150,000 signing bonus —huge for that time—to steer him away from the National Football League. Hoping he would develop into a catcher in the mold of Hall of Famers Bill Dickey and Yogi Berra, the Yankees ultimately were disappointed in Gibbs. He reached the majors in 1962 and played parts of 10 years in pinstripes, but he batted only .233 in 538 games with 25 homers and 146 RBIs. Only twice did he play in more than half the team's games, and he never played in a World Series.

Baseball came to the Old South in 1966, when the Braves moved from Milwaukee to Atlanta. Three Mississippians played for the Braves in their early years in the Georgia capital. Bob Didier of Hattiesburg was the starting catcher as a rookie for the 1969 team that won the first National League West Division championship. Laurel's Rod Gilbreath made it to Atlanta in 1972 and spent parts of seven years with the team, batting .248 in 500 games. In 1973, another Laurel native, Jack Pierce, arrived in Atlanta with the promise of being a big-time slugger. But he lasted just two years with the Braves and hit a grand total of eight homers in the majors.

~ ~ ~

In the year of the Pitcher, 1968, only one Mississippian was pitching in the big leagues. Hickory native Joe Gibbon, another former two-sport star (basketball and baseball) at Ole Miss, was 1-2 with a save and a 1.58 ERA as a reliever for San Francisco. His ERA was the best on the staff. In 1969, with the lower mound, the left-hander had a 3.60 ERA for the Giants before he was traded to Pittsburgh, where he went 5-1 with nine saves and a 1.94 mark. For his career, Gibbon posted a fine 3.52 ERA and he earned 61 wins in 419

145

games with four different teams. He was out of the game after the 1972 season.

The designated hitter rule was instituted in the American League in 1973, and several Mississippians took advantage of it to extend their careers. George Scott of Greenville, while being a good fielder, served as a DH at times, and Calhoun City's Dave Parker was used almost exclusively as a DH in Oakland in the latter stages of his career.

One player who seemed a natural for the DH role was Gulfport native Bill Melton. The 6-foot-2, 200-pound Melton blasted 89 homers in his first three full years in the majors, all with the Chicago White Sox. In 1971, he won the American League home run title on the last day of the season, belting his 33rd off Milwaukee's Bill Parsons before a tiny crowd of 2,814 at Comiskey Park. Melton tossed his batting helmet to the fans as he rounded third base and paid the man who caught the homer $50 for the ball.

"He told me it was the 490th ball he caught at the ballpark over the years," Melton remarked in Richard Lindberg's *Who's On Third?*, a history of the White Sox. "I asked him if he ever works."

But Melton fell into disfavor with White Sox faithful. He was never a good third baseman, and Harry Caray, then the White Sox radio man, harped constantly on Melton's shortcomings with the glove.

After his big year in 1971, Melton struggled with the insults and with injuries over the next four seasons —once striking out 10 straight times over a three-game stretch—before Chicago dealt him to the California Angels in 1976. As the regular DH for the Angels, he hit six homers that year. In 1977, he went to Cleveland and finished his career there as a little-used DH who failed to homer in 50 games. He finished with 160 homers (and 669 strikeouts) in 1,144 major league games.

"Those who live by the sword die by the sword. A herniated disc cut short his career, but Bill Melton might have lasted a bit longer if he had concentrated on making contact with the ball instead of swinging for the fences," Lindberg wrote.

The ultimate baseball specialist might have been Herb Washington, a Belzoni native who had been a track star at Michigan State before he was signed in 1974 by offbeat Oakland A's owner Charlie O. Finley to serve as a designated pinch runner. Washington had once held world indoor records in the 50- and 60-yard dashes, but he hadn't played baseball since high school. Maury Wills, once tutored by Starkville native Cool Papa Bell on the art of the steal, was brought in by the A's to work with "Hurricane Herb."

"Because his only job was base stealing—he never came to bat—he had about as much of an element of surprise as sunshine," Randy Rieland wrote in *The New Professionals*. "Opposing pitchers and catchers began plotting his demise from the moment he trotted out of the dugout."

Washington stole 28 bases in 45 tries, a poor percentage by any standard, and scored 29 runs in 1974. He was a frequent pick-off victim, including once in the World Series against the Los Angeles Dodgers. Washington was released early in 1975 season, having appeared in 13 games and swiped two bases. His career numbers: 105 games, 30 steals, zero at-bats. "I'd feel sorry for him," Oakland third baseman Sal Bando said, "if he were a player."

Finley did not abandon the idea of a designated pinch runner after the Washington experiment failed. Later in 1975, he brought up West Point native Don Hopkins for the same purpose. Hopkins lasted two years in the majors, stealing 21 bases and scoring 25 runs in 85 games. A true baseball player, he actually batted six times for A's and got a hit. Hopkins' big league career ended in 1976.

~ ~ ~

During this dynamic period of the game, a large number of Mississippians burst onto the major league scene. Among them were Dennis "Oil Can" Boyd (Meridian), Ellis Burks (Vicksburg), Dave Clark (Tupelo), Stan and Stew Cliburn (Jackson), Billy Cowan (Yazoo City), Tommy Dean (Iuka), Curtis Ford (Jackson), Charlie Hayes (Hattiesburg), Cleo James (Clarksdale), Barry Lyons (Biloxi), Gerry Moses (Yazoo City) and Fred Valentine (Clarksdale). Worthy of a special mention is Mickey Harrington, a Hattiesburg native and onetime Mississippi Southern (now USM) standout who pulled a Moonlight Graham in 1963, appearing in one game without getting to bat for the Philadelphia Phillies.

"It was a thrill to get there," said Harrington, who played 10 seasons of pro ball all told. "But it was a letdown not getting to bat. It would have been nice to bat one time."

But he could still call himself a major leaguer.

149

Baseball survived so many things in the 20th century: the Black Sox scandal and the Great Depression, war, political and social upheaval and even ghastly polyester uniforms. But when the 1994 season was abruptly halted by yet another player strike, one that resulted in the World Series being called off, the grand old game faced perhaps its biggest challenge. It had to win its fans back—and just when things seemed to be going really well, it was struck by another jolt of controversy.

Spotlight
Managerial Material

Only three Mississippians have ever managed in the major leagues, and all three, by odd coincidence, did so in Houston. None of the three, however, experienced great success. Ellisville native Harry Craft holds the distinction of having been the first manager of the Houston Colt .45s, a National League expansion team in 1962. He lasted almost three seasons, getting the ax with 13 games left in 1964. Craft, a fine outfielder in his playing days, had managed before, running the Kansas City Athletics for parts of three seasons in the late 1950s and the Chicago Cubs for 16 games in 1961. Craft's managerial record was 360-485, and he never experienced a winning season. He took over the A's late in 1957 and went 23-27 down the stretch. His best club was the '58 A's, who finished 73-81, good enough only for seventh place in the eight-team league. That team featured a young Roger Maris but not much else. Pascagoula's Harry Walker, who won two World Series rings and a batting title as a player, was the first Mississippi native to land a big league managing gig, taking over the St. Louis Cardinals as a player/manager in early 1955. The team finished 51-67 under Walker and he was canned. His next opportunity didn't come until 1965, when he took the reins in Pittsburgh. His first two teams went 90-72 and

92-70 but didn't win a pennant, and he was fired during the 1967 season. In 1968, Walker was hired by the Houston Astros (nee Colt .45s), whom he managed until 1972, when he was sacked in mid-season despite a 67-54 record. That was his final team. Walker's career record was 630-604, but he won no championships. Tupelo native Dave Clark, an outstanding pinch hitter in his playing days, was hired as interim manager by the Astros in 2009, moving from first-base coach to replace the fired Cecil Cooper. Clark guided the club to a 4-9 record. He was interviewed for the manager job after the season but it went to Brad Mills. Clark continued as a coach for the Astros and will always own the distinction of being the first black Mississippian to manage a big league team.

A Minor Tradition

With the arrival in Jackson, Mississippi, of the Double-A Texas League Mets, a New York Mets farm club, in 1975, a steady stream of players with newly minted Mississippi connections began to flow into the major league ranks, a trend that continued with the Generals (a Houston Astros affiliate) from 1991-99 and the Mississippi Braves, a Double-A Southern League club aligned with the Atlanta Braves that arrived in Pearl in 2005.

Former JaxMets such as Ron Gardenhire, Ned Yost, Dave Magadan and Roger McDowell were managing or coaching in the majors in 2011 and ex-Generals like Lance Berkman, Bobby Abreu, Melvin Mora and Freddy Garcia were still playing in 2011, serving as a constant reminder of Mississippi's minor league history.

But the state's minor league tradition runs much deeper than those Double-A clubs. Devoted baseball fans in Mississippi know the names Bill Dickey, Billy Herman and Walter Alston. They might not know that each of those National Baseball Hall of Famers played minor league ball in Mississippi.

Lesser known but no less significant in the state's minor league history are such players as Banks "The Walking Man" McDowell, Deo "The Whistling First Baseman" Grose and Tom McBride. They were stars on the Jackson Senators teams of the 1940s.

Jackson is one of 19 Mississippi cities that have had professional baseball clubs. The capital city's minor league roots can be traced back to 1904, almost to the birth of the National Association of Professional Baseball Leagues, the organization formed in 1901 that is now known simply as Minor League Baseball.

For every Darryl Strawberry, Billy Wagner and Brian McCann— products of the Jackson area Double-A clubs—there's an Ed Greer, Horace Long and Tommy Davis. Obscure names today, they were the glory of their times. Greer won 23 games for Jackson's 1927 club. Long blasted a league-leading 17 homers for Jackson in 1931. Davis led the league with a .341 batting average and 125 RBIs in 1948.

Contemporary Jackson-area fans can brag about the league championships won by the JaxMets in 1981, 1984 and 1985, the Generals' titles of 1993 and 1996, or the M-Braves' pennant in 2008. But an older generation of cranks could regale you with tales of the Southeastern League champion Senators of 1940 or 1947.

Jackson teams played in six different minor leagues before the Texas League club arrived. The first Jackson team, in 1904, played in the Class D Delta League, a low-level circuit. Then there was the Cotton States League, the Mississippi State League, the Dixie League, the East Dixie League and the Southeastern League. Other Mississippi cities had teams in those leagues and in others such as the Tri-State League and the Evangeline League.

"The old Cotton States League created a lot of interest around the state," said Boo Ferriss, the former major league pitcher from Shaw. "A lot of guys from that league went on up to the big leagues. I followed a lot of them when I was a kid."

Tom McBride arrived in Jackson in 1937, when the team was in the Class B Southeastern League. He played the outfield for the Senators for parts of the next five years before eventually moving up to the majors for tours with the Boston Red Sox and Washington Senators. McBride was part of an outfield in 1937 that also consisted of former University of Tennessee football star Beattie Feathers and future Pro Football Hall of Famer Don Hutson.

"I had more fun in Jackson than at any time playing pro ball," McBride said. "We loved it there, my wife and I."

The Senators went into hiatus during the wars years of 1943-45 but were revived in 1946 as a farm club of the Boston Braves. Vern Bickford, who won 11 games for the pennant-winning Braves in 1948, pitched for the 1946 Senators. The club folded in 1950 only to be revived again in 1953. But on Aug. 8 of that year, a tornado destroyed League Park, the fairgrounds facility where the Senators played, and the team finished out the season playing all road games. The park wasn't rebuilt, and the team never came back.

The entire Cotton States League folded in 1955, leaving Mississippi without a professional baseball team until the New York Mets relocated their Double-A club to newly constructed Smith-Wills Stadium in 1975. The JaxMets produced a bountiful number of major leaguers —Lee Mazzili, Jeff Reardon, Mookie Wilson, Darryl Strawberry, Kevin Mitchell, Lenny Dykstra, Gregg Jefferies, Todd Hundley, et. Al—before leaving in 1990 because of a dispute over stadium renovations. The

Houston Astros moved in the next season, and a new pipeline to the majors was opened.

During the mid-1990s, independent baseball—not affiliated with Major League Baseball—enjoyed a revival in the state, with several cities, including Greenville, Meridian and Tupelo, fielding teams in various leagues.

After the Astros left Jackson in 1999 (the franchise was sold by local owner Con Maloney because of rising costs and declining attendance), two different independent clubs followed as Smith-Wills Stadium tenants. The Diamond Kats, of the Texas-Louisiana League, lasted just one year. A new incarnation of the Senators was born in 2002 as part of the Central Baseball League, a revamped version of the Tex-La League. The Senators won a championship in 2003. They played their last season in 2005, essentially driven from the area by the arrival that year of the Mississippi Braves, an affiliated club that moved into $30 million Trustmark Park in Pearl.

The M-Braves almost immediately began churning out major league talent. Catcher Brian McCann was the first to be called to Atlanta in June of 2005. "He could be there 15 days or 15 years," said Brian Snitker, the M-

Braves manager that season. McCann never played another day in the minors, quickly becoming an All-Star. He was followed to The Show by pitcher Blaine Boyer and then outfielder Jeff Francoeur, who had such an impact that he made the cover of *Sports Illustrated* that summer. Through the 2011 season, their seventh in Pearl, the M-Braves had shepherded more than 50 players to the major leagues.

By Any Other Name

Baseball nicknames have a certain charm unique to the sport. There are no Destroyers or Meat Cleavers, Assassins or Undertakers. Baseball nicknames have a kinder, gentler quality.

Baseball has given us Spuds, Motormouth, Big Unit and Penguin. Long before television sportscaster Chris Berman came up with contrived monikers such as Bert "Be Home" Blyleven and Bernard "Innocent Until Proven" Gilkey, baseball had Shoeless Joe Jackson, Highpockets Kelly, Mordecai "Three Finger" Brown and Frankie "The Fordham Flash" Frisch.

Lenny Dykstra was just plain Lenny when he played for Jackson's minor league Mets in 1984. When he got to the big leagues shortly thereafter, the scrappy, tobacco-spitting Dykstra came to be known as "Nails." A perfect fit. Another Jackson Mets alumnus, journeyman catcher Doug Gwosdz, was bestowed a nickname that belongs on any all-time list: Eyechart.

If there were a Nickname Hall of Fame in baseball, Mississippians could fill an entire wing. Players from the Magnolia State seem to attract colorful monikers.

Here's a top 10 list:

1. Dennis "Oil Can" Boyd.
2. James "Cool Papa" Bell.
3. Harry "The Hat" Walker.
4. Gerald "Gee" Walker.
5. George "Boomer" Scott.
6. Guy "The Mississippi Mudcat" Bush.
7. Atley "Swampy" Donald.
8. Don "The Corinth Comet" Blasingame.
9. Bob "The Rope" Boyd.
10. Eric "Boob" McNair.

Honorable mention goes to Harry "Popeye" Craft (also tagged "Wildfire" for a time), Chris "The Tin Man" Brown, Dave "Boo" Ferriss, Fred "Squeaky" Valentine and Wilmer "Vinegar Bend" Mizell, a Leakesville native whose odd moniker was taken from an Alabama community in which he played amateur ball.

Some of these require an explanation.

Meridian native Boyd's nickname had something to do with beer, which he and his boyhood friends called "oil." The nickname apparently did not derive from any similarities between Boyd and Oil Can Harry, the villainous cat from the old Mighty Mouse cartoons, though that might have been appropriate.

Boyd seemed to attract trouble throughout a star-crossed 10-year big league career. A skinny right-hander with a big leg kick, he won 78 games, 43 of those during a fairly brilliant three-year span (1984-86) with the Boston Red Sox. He won 16 games for the BoSox in 1986 and pitched in that year's World Series, which Boston lost in heart-wrenching fashion to the New York Mets.

During the 1986 season, Boyd threw a much-publicized tantrum over being snubbed from the All-Star Game, drew a suspension from the club, got arrested and was ordered to see a psychiatrist. Soon after that, he began to develop shoulder problems that hastened the end of his big league career. His last major league appearance was in 1991, but he would pitch in independent baseball for several years after that and even spoke of attempting a comeback in 2009 at the age of 50.

In *The Ballplayers*, a biographical reference work published in 1990, the Dennis Boyd entry starts like this: "One of 14 children of former Negro Leaguer Willie James Boyd, the flamboyant, moody, and high-strung Oil Can is one of baseball's underachievers, plagued by a hot temper and persistent shoulder problems. … (H)e became disliked around the league for his cocky demeanor and animated fist-pumping and finger-wagging on the mound."

Boyd said he was just misunderstood in Boston, the result of a culture clash.

"They said I was bitter about the way I grew up," said Boyd, who came during the racial turbulence of the 1960s and 1970s. "But that wasn't true. I just wanted people to understand where I was coming from. But I was always fingered as being wrong."

If nothing else, Boyd will always be remembered for his nickname, which could be said for many Mississippians.

Negro Leagues star Bell, a Hall of Famer from Starkville, was called "Cool" by his teammates because of the poise he displayed at a young age. As the story goes, "Papa" was tacked on because it sounded better. Cool Papa Bell Drive, the entrance road to the Mississippi Sports Hall of Fame and Smith-Wills Stadium in Jackson is named in Bell's honor.

Harry Walker, from Pascagoula, was nicknamed "The Hat" because of his habit of tugging on the bill of his cap while standing in the batter's box.

Greenville's Scott was known as "Boomer" for his prodigious home runs—"taters," he called them. Corinth native Blasingame was called "Comet" or "Blazer" because of his baserunning skills; in seven of his 12 seasons he had seven or more triples. Bob Boyd, from Potts Camp, hit so many line drives—.293 career hitter —he came to be nicknamed "The Rope." Meridian native McNair was called "Possum" when he first arrived in the big leagues in 1929 but also acquired the nickname "Boob," allegedly because he bore a resemblance to a cartoon strip character of the period named Boob McNutt.

Gerald Walker, a Gulfport native who played at Ole Miss in 1920s, was called "Gee" for much of his big league career. But "Gee" wasn't short for Gerald. He got his nickname from an on-field incident. Coaching first base in a game, he apparently neglected to tell a runner to hold up at the bag after a hit. The runner was thrown out, and Walker's angry manager demanded an explanation. Walker defended himself, saying he had yelled "Gee! Gee!" In Walker's country boy parlance, "Haw" was what you yelled to a mule if you wanted it to go to the left. "Gee" was what you yelled if you wanted the mule to go to the right. When Walker yelled "Gee" at the base runner, he was trying to tell him to curl off to the right and not try for second base.

Another great baseball nickname was born.

Chapter 5

Power Ball
1995-Present

Jackson, Mississippi native Chad Bradford
appeared in 561 big league games
(Photo courtesy of University of Southern Mississippi)

On the World Stage

The ball curled high off the bat of the Atlanta Braves' Mark Lemke and drifted beyond the left-field foul line, toward the seats at Yankee Stadium. New York's third baseman, Charlie Hayes, gave chase. The ball plopped into his glove. Hayes thrust his arms skyward and began to jump for joy. Yankee Stadium went nuts, and so did Hayes' teammates.

The Yankees had just won the 1996 World Series, ending an 18-year championship drought for the major leagues' most celebrated franchise.

Hattiesburg native Hayes played parts of 14 seasons in the big leagues for seven different teams, batting .262 with 144 home runs and enjoying many a shining moment. But the catch that ended the 1996 Series was different. That season was different.

"Winning the World Series with the Yankees was the highlight of my career," said Hayes, who played only 262 of his 1,547 career games with the Bronx Bombers. "People remember me with the Yankees. It was the most fun I had playing ball."

The Yankees had won 27 World Series championships through 2011, far and away the most of any major league club. Yankees fans expect to win.

Yankees management spends big money toward that end. Players feel the expectations.

"I played with a lot of teams, but the aura of the Yankees … Yankee Stadium … there's no other stadium like it," Hayes said. "I don't know how to describe it. It's so different, just a whole different atmosphere. I remember the first time I walked out there. It's unbelievable, overwhelming."

Hayes didn't have a great Series in 1996—batting just .188 while playing in five of the six games. But he got a ring, which is the goal, stated or unstated, of every player who makes it to the major leagues.

New Albany native Eli Whiteside, a backup catcher for San Francisco, didn't play in the 2010 World Series against Texas, but he got a ring when the Giants won their first championship since moving from New York in 1958. Ellis Burks, from Vicksburg, played just a handful of games for Boston in 2004—his final season—and wasn't on the roster by the time the Red Sox reached the Fall Classic against St. Louis.

But Burks, originally drafted by Boston in 1983, was rewarded with a ring after Boston ended its legendary title drought that stretched back to 1918. Meridian native Jay Powell pitched a scoreless top of the

167

11th inning in Game 7 of the 1997 Series and got the win
—and a ring—when the Florida Marlins beat Cleveland
on an Edgar Renteria hit in the bottom of the 11th.

World Series performances such as those become
indelible memories. To wit: Jackson's Seth Smith was a
rookie with the Colorado Rockies in 2007 when he made
the last out of the Series against Boston; the former Ole
Miss star was struck out by Jonathan Papelbon, a former
Mississippi State pitcher.

One of the best Series performances by a
Mississippi-born player came in 1985, when
Greenville's Frank White helped the Kansas City Royals
win their first championship. Best known for his glove
work at second base, White hit .250, scored four times
and drove in six runs as the Royals beat St. Louis in
seven games. Kansas City lost the first two games of that
series, at home, but turned things around in Game 3,
winning 6-1 with the aid of a clutch home run by White.
"We went into St. Louis trying to win two games so we
could get the series back to Kansas City and go for
broke," he told *USA Today*. They did, winning Games 6
and 7 at home. Royals pitcher Bret Saberhagen won the
MVP award, but White certainly made valuable
contributions.

Mississippians have produced a mixed bag of highlights and pratfalls in the Fall Classic going back to 1917, when Jackson native Reb Russell became the first from the Magnolia State to play on baseball's biggest stage.

The 1917 Series was knotted at 2-games all when Russell, a 28-year-old left-hander, was handed the ball to start Game 5 for the Chicago White Sox against the New York Giants. A 15-game winner during the regular season, Russell couldn't find his command on that October day at Comiskey Park. He faced three batters and retired none. He was hastily replaced by Ed Cicotte, who had worked eight innings just three days earlier.

The Giants scored twice in the first inning, but the Sox came back to win 8-5. Two days later, Chicago claimed the Series with a win in Game 6. Russell's one and only World Series appearance was truly forgettable —but he got a championship ring.

So did Herb Washington, a Belzoni native and erstwhile track star who served as a "designated runner" for the Oakland A's in 1974 when they reached the World Series and faced the Los Angeles Dodgers. Washington had some success as a base stealer during the season, but his one appearance in the Series was a disaster. Inserted as a pinch runner at first base in the ninth inning of Game 2, Washington was picked off by the Dodgers' Mike Marshall. The A's lost the game but went on to win the Series in five. Washington got a ring.

In the 1960 Series, Wilmer "Vinegar Bend" Mizell of Leakesville had an experience similar to Reb Russell's. Mizell started Game 3 for Pittsburgh against the New York Yankees and was knocked out in the first inning, in which New York scored six runs en route to a 10-0 victory. Mizell worked in relief in Game 6 and pitched two scoreless innings in a game the Yankees would win 12-0. But he got a championship ring, thanks to Bill Mazeroski's game-ending home run in the ninth inning of Game 7.

The Pirates also won a world championship in 1979, with a Mississippi native playing a more prominent role. Calhoun City's Dave Parker, a big, brash right fielder, hit .345 with four RBIs as Pittsburgh topped Baltimore in seven games. Parker, who had batted .310 with 25 homers during the regular season, got the game-winning hit in Game 6. He would appear in two more Fall Classics, earning a second ring in 1989 as a member of the Oakland A's, who beat San Francisco in the earthquake-interrupted Series.

Aberdeen's Guy Bush pitched the only win the Chicago Cubs managed in the 1929 World Series against the powerful Philadelphia A's, and he also appeared in the 1932 Series loss against the New York Yankees, a showdown made famous by Babe Ruth's alleged called-shot home run.

Gee Walker of Gulfport, playing for the Detroit Tigers, had a game-tying pinch-hit double in the ninth inning of Game 2 of the 1934 Series against St. Louis. The game went 12 innings, and the Tigers won it 3-2. But the Gas House Gang Cardinals won the Series in seven.

Weir's Roy Oswalt pitched Houston to its first World Series appearance in 2005—winning MVP honors in the National League Championship Series—but the Astros were dismissed in four games by the Chicago White Sox.

Morton native Atley Donald was involved in one of the Fall Classic's most famous—or perhaps infamous—games. It happened in 1941, in the fourth game of the Series between Donald's Yankees and the Brooklyn Dodgers. Donald, New York's No. 5 starter most of that season, drew the start at Brooklyn's Ebbets Field. The hard-throwing right-hander had beaten Cleveland

Indians ace Bob Feller twice during the season, so Yankees manager Joe McCarthy had confidence in giving Donald the ball with New York up 2-1 in the Series. Donald was given an early 3-0 lead but couldn't hold it. Brooklyn pounded him for six hits and four runs in his four-plus innings and took a 4-3 lead to the ninth. Donald stood to get the loss when disaster struck the Dodgers.

Brooklyn was one strike away from a crucial victory that would have tied the Series when a third-strike curveball thrown by Hugh Casey eluded Dodgers catcher Mickey Owen. Tommy Henrich, the batter, reached first base on the most notorious passed ball in baseball history and kept the Yankees' faint hopes alive. And then it all caved in on Brooklyn. Boom, boom, boom. Just that quickly, the Yankees scored four times before Brooklyn could get the third out in the ninth. Ebbets Field fell silent. The Dodgers were retired meekly in the bottom of the ninth. The Yankees won 7-4. They took the 3-1 Series lead back to the Bronx and captured the championship the next day.

Four years later, in the war-diluted 1945 World Series between the Chicago Cubs and Detroit Tigers — some wags of the day claimed neither team was good enough to win it—Waynesboro native Claude Passeau pitched a magnificent one-hit shutout in Game 3 to give the Cubs a 2-1 Series lead. Passeau made two more appearances and posted a 2.70 ERA in 16 2/3 innings overall. But his contributions were not enough to stave off the Tigers, who won in seven games.

In the classic 1946 Series between the St. Louis Cardinals and Boston Red Sox—featuring legendary sluggers Stan Musial and Ted Williams—unheralded Harry Walker of Gulfport hit .412 with six RBIs in the seven games and drove in Enos Slaughter with what proved to be the Series-clinching run in the eighth inning of Game 7. Shaw native Boo Ferriss threw a six-hit shutout for the Red Sox in that Series and started Game 7, but he was on the bench by the time Walker got his big hit.

The Red Sox's appearance in the 1946 Series was the franchise's first since it won the 1918 championship. Boston owner Harry Frazee, needing cash, traded star pitcher Babe Ruth to the New York Yankees the next year, launching the dynasty in the Bronx and placing an apparent hex on the Red Sox.

The so-called "Curse of the Bambino" lasted until 2004, when Boston claimed an improbable

173

championship, beating the Yankees along the way. The Red Sox lost seven-game Series in 1946, 1967, 1975 and 1986 before that breakthrough.

Greenville native George Scott was on the 1967 Boston club; he hit .231 without an RBI in the Series loss to the St. Louis Cardinals. Meridian's Oil Can Boyd, a 16-game winner for Boston in 1986, had a rough outing in Game 3 of that year's Series—six runs in seven innings of a 7-1 loss—and was passed over for a scheduled start in Game 7, which followed Boston's infamous collapse in Game 6, the one immortalized by Bill Buckner's error at first base. Bruce Hurst started the seventh game for the Red Sox, and they lost 8-5. Boyd never got into the game.

"Boyd was inconsolable both before and after the game," Ron Fimrite reported in *Sports Illustrated*. "'I wanted the call,' said the Can, sobbing in front of his locker. 'but I didn't get the call.'" Boyd would never get so close to a ring again.

Power Ball

This has been a tumultuous period for baseball, an era marked by assaults on hallowed home run records and the advent of drug testing. Wild card teams were introduced in a newly expanded postseason. Interleague play began, popular with many fans if not the purists.

The annual All-Star Game was given new significance as the determiner of home-field advantage in the World Series, another controversial decision. One constant remained: Mississippi natives continued to make their presence felt.

As baseball sought to recover from the eight-month work stoppage that wiped out the 1994 World Series and disrupted the start of the 1995 season, Cal Ripken's inexorable march toward Lou Gehrig's consecutive games streak helped bring fans back to the game. But something else began to happen that captured the fancy of the masses baseball feared it had lost: Balls began flying out of ballparks at an incredible rate.

On May 28, 1995, in a game between Chicago and Detroit, a record 12 home runs were struck. During the 1996 season, major league players hit 4,962 homers, the most in 128 years of professional baseball. A record 43 players hit 30 or more homers that season, and a record 17 hit 40 or more. The Colorado Rockies had three players hit the 40 mark, becoming just the second team ever to accomplish that feat; one of those three was Vicksburg native Ellis Burks, who produced perhaps the best season ever by a Mississippi-born player.

Burks hit 40 of his career 352 homers in that 1996 season as a member of the Rockies' so-called Blake Street Bombers. The then 32-year-old outfielder also batted .344, drove in 128 runs, scored a National League-leading 142 runs, slugged an National League-best .639 and, on top of that, stole 32 bases. He became only the second player in history—Hank Aaron was the first—to amass at least 200 hits, 40 homers and 30 steals in a single season. Burks finished third in the National League MVP voting in '96.

At least some part of the home run explosion could be explained by the emergence of new, more hitter-friendly ballparks, a trend kicked off by the construction of Camden Yards in Baltimore in 1992. But at the same time, players were getting noticeably bigger and stronger, the byproduct, it appeared, of extensive weight training and the use of dietary supplements such as

Creatine, an over-the-counter product that was plentiful in major league clubhouses by the mid-1990s.

"Like never before, baseball is about being buff. Anybody hoping to get to the World Series had better come to play with plenty of muscle and plenty of money. Better to have too much than not enough," Tom Verducci wrote in a *Sports Illustrated* article.

In 1998, both Mark McGwire and Sammy Sosa, sporting comic-book hero physiques, surpassed Roger Maris' 1961 single-season home run record of 61, McGwire finishing with 70 bombs and Sosa with 66. Maybe we should have seen this coming.

"(T)he arrival of the (expansion) Devil Rays and Diamondbacks has forced into service 22 pitchers who should be either retired or in the minors," Verducci wrote. "The impact is predictable. In each of the past five expansion years, there were nearly uniform increases in home runs, batting average, walks and ERA, with dingers going up the most on average. The results will be even more dramatic this season, not only because this is the second expansion within six years but also because the hitters have never been stronger or more power-conscious."

The power surge didn't stop in 1998. More jaw-dropping feats would follow. Barry Bonds would set yet another single-season home run mark with 73 in 2001 as he moved ever closer to the career home run record, Hank Aaron's 755, which Bonds surpassed in 2007. On July 2, 2002—call it National Tater Day—a record 62 home runs were hit in big league games.

There were a record-tying 12 in the Detroit-Chicago game, and Mississippi natives Dmitri Young (Vicksburg) and Wendell Magee (Hattiesburg) contributed three of those as members of the Tigers. Young hit two and Magee one.

Young, who arrived in the majors in 1996 with St. Louis, personified power. Nicknamed "Da Meat Hook," he reportedly weighed as much as 300 pounds during the latter stages of his career, which was marred by injuries and off-field issues and ended in 2008. But when he could play, he could hit. Young batted .292 for his career and made two All-Star teams. And yet power is what he might best be remembered for. Among his 171 career homers were the three he struck on opening day at spacious Comerica Park in 2005 (something only one other player has ever done) and the 29 he smashed in his best season, 2003, when he played in a career-high 155 games for the Tigers.

Marcus Thames, a Louisville native, arrived in the majors with the New York Yankees in 2002 and did so with one impressive show of muscle. On June 10, in Yankee Stadium, on the first pitch he saw in the majors, Thames hit a towering home run off the Arizona Diamondbacks' Randy Johnson, one of the most feared left-handed hurlers of all-time. Though he rarely played regularly in a career that was still going in 2011, Thames made his mark with the long ball. During a seven-game stretch in 2008 while with Detroit, he hit seven home runs. Back with the Yankees in 2010, he hit six bombs in a six-game stretch. Through the 2010 season, Thames had 113 homers, a rate of one per every 15.4 at-bats, among the best ratios in history. (Mark McGwire hit one every 10.6 at-bats, Babe Ruth one every 11.8.)

Bill Hall, still playing in 2011, wasn't built like a home run hitter (6 feet, 210 pounds), but the Nettleton product did have one monster season, belting 35 homers for Milwaukee in 2006. During that year, he hit one of the most memorable homers ever by a Mississippi native. It was Mother's Day, and many players around the majors were using pink bats as part of a national breast cancer awareness campaign. Hall's mother, Vergie, had made the 10-hour drive from Nettleton to Milwaukee to see her son play. In the bottom of the 10th inning, with the Brewers trailing 5-4, Hall crushed a game-winning two-run home run off the New York Mets' Chad Bradford, another Mississippian from Byram.

"She's the love of my life," Hall told *The Associated Press*, referring to his mom, "so anything I can do special for her, I'm always up for it."

Fans everywhere, not just Bill Hall's mom, seemed to be "digging the long ball," to borrow a phrase from a popular TV commercial of the late 1990s. Major league attendance dropped, on average per game, from 1994 to 1995, but it began a three-year climb in 1996. After a slight dip in 1999, it rose again in 2000 and 2001. But by the time Bonds set his single-season homer record in 2001, a cloud had gathered over the game. Allegations were rampant that many players, hitters and pitchers, were using illegal performance-enhancing drugs (PEDs), including steroids and human growth hormone (HGH). Major League Baseball did not test for such drugs.

In a groundbreaking article published in June of 2002, *Sports Illustrated's* Verducci spelled out the dangers of PEDs and reported allegations from former players—most notably Ken Caminiti—about their widespread use in baseball. He wrote: "Steroids have helped create the greatest extended era of sluggers the game has ever seen—and, not coincidentally, the highest rate of strikeouts in history. Power, the eye candy for the casual fan, is a common denominator among pitchers and hitters, as hurlers, too, juice up to boost the velocity of their pitches."

Spurred by the controversy, Major League Baseball, finally gaining the consent of the powerful players' union, began "survey testing" for steroids in 2003 and revamped the program in 2004 and 2005. In March of 2005, Congress summoned several current and former players to Washington for a hearing on drug abuse in MLB. Among those appearing were McGwire, Sosa and former Mississippi State star Rafael Palmeiro, who dramatically wagged his finger while emphatically denying having ever using steroids.

Twelve players were suspended under MLB's 2005 drug-testing policy, including Palmeiro—shortly after he got his 3,000[th] career hit—and Gulfport native Matt

Lawton, who had enjoyed a fine career that even landed him an appearance on the cover of *Sports Illustrated* in 2001.

Palmeiro failed a test in August of 2005 while with the Baltimore Orioles and served a 10-game suspension. That would turn out to be his final season. Palmeiro publicly blamed the positive test on a tainted vitamin B-12 injection and has steadfastly denied using PEDs. But in the 2011 Baseball Hall of Fame voting, Palmeiro, one of only four players to have both 500 career homers and 3,000 career hits, was named on only 11 percent of the ballots, far short of the 75 percent needed for election. He made only small gains on the 2012 ballot.

Lawton failed a test late in 2005 and was suspended for the first 10 games of the 2006 season. He publicly acknowledged use of PEDs and apologized in a statement issued to *The Associated Press*. He played in 11 games for Seattle in 2006 before his release in May. That was the end of a 12-year career that saw him hit .267 with 138 homers and 631 RBIs. Only twice did Lawton hit as many as 20 homers in a season.

Baseball's battle against its image problems continued in 2006 when commissioner Bud Selig commissioned former U.S. Senator George Mitchell to investigate drug abuse in the game and the effectiveness of the drug-testing program. The report was made public in December of 2007, and 89 players, some retired, some active, were cited as having some kind of connection to steroids or other PEDs.

Exavier "Nook" Logan, from Natchez, was the only Mississippi native named in the report, though several former Jackson Mets minor leaguers and three Mississippi college alumni, including Palmeiro, were cited. Logan admitted to and apologized for HGH use, but he never played in the big leagues again after the 2007 season. Known much more for his speed than power, he hit .268 with a grand total of two homers in parts of four seasons in the majors.

By 2010, baseball appeared to be a cleaner game, a more balanced game. The crazy power numbers of the so-called Steroid Era had diminished.

Home run totals dropped in four straight seasons beginning in 2007. There were 1,080 fewer homers hit in 2010 than in 2000. Only two players reached the 40-homer plateau in 2010.

Major league teams scored 21,308 runs in 2010 — 1,111 less than in 2009 and the lowest total in the game since 1992. Pitching enjoyed a resurgence; 57 hurlers posted an ERA of 4.00 or less, the most since 1992. Speed and defense were back in the equation for success.

And fans have kept coming out. MLB set season attendance records for three straight years beginning in 2005. Though the figures dipped each of the next three seasons in a tough economic climate, baseball was enjoying greater popularity attendance-wise than it had at any time during the so-called Steroid Era (1995-2003).

The game always bounces back.

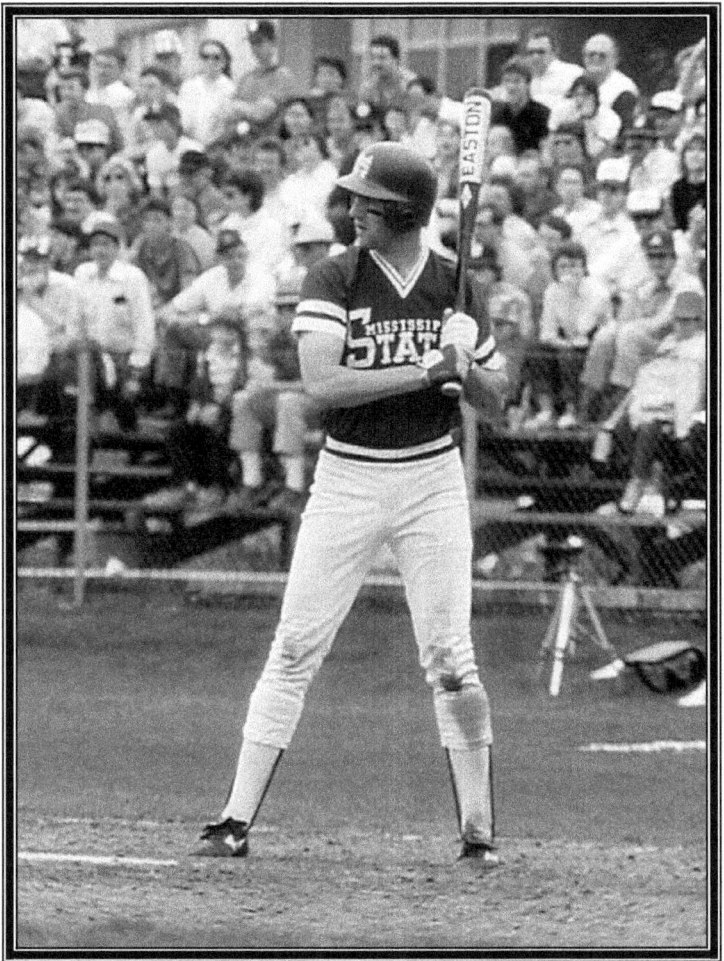

**Will Clark, a Louisiana native, starred for Mississippi
State's 1985College World Series team
(Courtesy Mississippi State University)**

College Boys

When the topic is Best College Team in Mississippi History, which covers a lot of very fertile ground, the debate pretty much begins and ends with the 1985 Mississippi State Bulldogs.

That team, coached by the incomparable Ron Polk, is the gold standard, not just for what it accomplished as a unit but also for what many members of that club went on to do in the professional ranks. It was an amazing collection of talent.

MSU did not win a national championship in 1985; through 2011, no Mississippi NCAA Division I school had managed that feat. (NAIA member William Carey won a national title in 1969, and NCAA Division II Delta State pulled it off in 2004.) The Bulldogs tied for third in the 1985 College World Series. After winning their first two games in Omaha, Nebraska, the Bulldogs lost to Texas and then squandered a lead against Miami (Florida), ending their season at 50-15.

Will Clark, a brash first baseman from New Orleans, was the lead dog on the 1985 MSU team. He hit .420 with 25 home runs and 77 RBIs, claiming the Golden Spikes Award, the college baseball equivalent of football's Heisman Trophy. Rafael Palmeiro, a Cuba native who grew up in the Miami area, played the Sundance Kid to Clark's Butch Cassidy. Palmeiro hit 20 homers and drove in 57 runs in 1985. Bobby Thigpen, from Florida, was a two-way star, playing right field and serving as the closer in tight games. Jeff Brantley, from Alabama, was the ace of the pitching staff, posting an 18-2 record with a 2.29 ERA (a remarkable figure in the era of high-powered metal bats).

Those four and three other Bulldogs were selected in the Major League Baseball draft in June of 1985, and the four stars would go on to have outstanding big league careers.

Thigpen, used exclusively as a pitcher in the pros, set an American League saves record (since broken) with 57 in 1990 with the Chicago White Sox. He finished with 201 career saves, a 31-36 record and a 3.43 ERA over nine seasons in The Show. Brantley appeared in 615 big league games, mostly as a reliever, over 14 years. He finished with a 43-46 record, 172 saves and a 3.39 ERA. Clark broke into the majors with a home run off of the great Nolan Ryan and went on to hit 283 more round-trippers over a 15-year career. He hit .303 and made six All-Star teams.

Palmeiro's career totals outshone those of the other three. He played 20 big league seasons and finished with 569 home runs and 3,020 hits, becoming only the fourth player in history to reach both of those milestones. Palmeiro's career was tainted in 2005, his final season, when he failed an Major League Baseball drug test and was suspended for 10 games. Though his numbers would appear Hall of Fame worthy, he came up well short in the voting in 2010, the first time he was eligible for election.

Polk served two stints as MSU's coach, winning 1,139 games in 28 seasons there, and is credited by many with helping to elevate college baseball, both in Mississippi and across the country, to the unprecedented popularity it now enjoys.

MSU has produced a wealth of major league players over the years; Mitch Moreland became the 45th former Bulldogs player to make it to that level when he was called up by the Texas Rangers in 2010. Among the other MSU alumni with significant big league time are Hughie Critz, Sammy Ellis, Boo Ferriss, Alex Grammas, Paul Maholm, Jonathan Papelbon and Del Unser.

Ole Miss, too, has been a productive factory for major league talent. Eight former Rebels appeared in the big leagues in 2011: Chris Coghlan, Zack Cozart, Lance Lynn, Matt Maloney, Drew Pomeranz, Alex Presley, Seth Smith and Matt Tolbert. The Ole Miss' all-time list includes David Dellucci, Jeff Fassero, Joe Gibbon, Jake Gibbs, Don Kessinger, Bobby Kielty and Gee and Hub Walker.

Jim Davenport, a longtime stalwart with the San Francisco Giants, tops the list of former Southern Mississippi standouts who reached the majors. Others include Chad Bradford (featured prominently in the 2011 movie *Moneyball*), Bubba Phillips, Pat Rapp and Kevin Young.

Mississippi's smaller schools have gotten in on the act, as well. Jackson State helped groom the likes of Dave Clark, Oil Can Boyd, Curtis Ford and Marvin Freeman for major league careers. Division II Delta State, where Boo Ferriss became a coaching legend, had four alumni in the majors at one time during the 2009 season: catcher Eli Whiteside, infielder Edwin Maysonet and pitchers Dusty Hughes and Brent Leach. And 10 players who cut their teeth in Mississippi's junior college system played in the majors in 2011. That list included Philadelphia Phillies ace left-hander Cliff Lee, who played at Meridian Community College, as well as

Mississippi Gulf Coast CC's Fred Lewis and Tony Sipp, Itawamba CC's Desmond Jennings and Tim Dillard and East Central CC product Marcus Thames.

Welcome to The Show

There were three compelling stories involving Mississippi natives in the major leagues in 2010. Ironically, in a season that came to be known as "The Year of the Pitcher," all three stories involved position players.

Jarrod Dyson, an outfielder from McComb, made his major league debut just four years after being selected in the 50th and final round of the first-year player draft. John Lindsey, a first baseman out of Hattiesburg, made his major league debut 15 long years after playing in his first professional game. And Mitch Moreland, a first baseman/outfielder from Amory, was called up to the majors for the first time at the end of July and made significant contributions in the Texas Rangers' march to their first World Series appearance.

Speed, which might be gaining a renewed appreciation in what looks like a new era in the major leagues, is what carried Dyson to The Show. He stole

131 bases in 162 attempts in the minors. The 5-foot-9, 160-pound Dyson debuted for the Kansas City Royals on Sept. 7, drew a walk as a pinch hitter and scored a run. The next night, used as a pinch runner, he stole a base. On Sept. 21, starting in center field, he put on quite a show against Detroit. He doubled twice, singled once, drew a walk, put down a sacrifice bunt, scored three times, knocked in a run and stole a base. The Royals won 9-6.

"When I get on base, I can create havoc," Dyson told the *Kansas City Star*. Added his manager, former Jackson Mets catcher Ned Yost, "The thing I like about him is, you can't play him short in the outfield, either. He can drive the ball. He's an interesting little guy."

Dyson hit just .211 in his rookie season but stole nine bases in 18 games and was back on the Royals' opening day roster in 2011, though he would spent most of the season at the Triple-A level.

Lindsey made his big league debut on Sept. 8 with the Los Angeles Dodgers. After 1,571 games and 5,597 at-bats in the minors, the 33-year-old Lindsey was called on to pinch hit against San Diego at the Padres' Petco Park. Then cruel fate intervened. The Padres changed pitchers, bringing in a right-hander to face Lindsey, an imposing 6-foot-2, 255-pound right-handed hitter who had 219 minor league homers on his resume.

The Dodgers countered by pinch-hitting for Lindsey. He had to wait yet another day for his first at-bat; he would fly out as a pinch hitter. He got 11 more at-bats for the Dodgers but managed just one hit before his season was ended by a broken hand, suffered when he was hit by a pitch. Still on the major league roster for spring training in 2011, Lindsey was sent back to the minors in late March.

Lindsey was drafted out of Hattiesburg High by the Colorado Rockies in 1995. Over the years he would play for 13 different minor league clubs, including two stints in independent ball. He had decided to retire after the 2006 season but was talked into giving it another try by a minor league manager in the Dodgers' system. He played on for four more years before getting the call that every minor leaguer craves, this particular one from L.A. general manager Ned Colletti. "You reward people for the right reasons, including heart," Colletti told ESPNLosAngeles.com.

Moreland's rookie season in the big leagues had a fairy tale quality. A 17th-round pick by the Rangers out of Mississippi State in 2007, he established himself as a top prospect in 2009, when he hit .326 at Double-A Frisco and was named the Rangers' minor league player of the year. He was hitting .289 with 12 homers at Triple-A Oklahoma City when Texas summoned him to the majors in the heat of the American League pennant race. Moreland went 2-for-4 in his debut on July 29.

"This is what I've always wanted to do, since I could walk," Moreland said. "I started playing T-ball at 5 years old. I've played ever since."

Moreland played 47 games for the Rangers down the stretch, mostly at first base or in right field, and hit .255 with nine home runs and 25 RBIs. The Rangers won the American League West. In the playoffs, the lefty-swinging Moreland really found his groove, batting .348 with a homer and seven RBIs. Though Texas lost to San Francisco in five games in the World Series, Moreland went 6-for-15 against the Giants' vaunted pitching staff. His postseason homer came in Game 3, the only one the Rangers won. "To experience the postseason in your first year, you can't ask for much more than that," Moreland told the author.

Amory held a Mitch Moreland Day on Dec. 10, 2010, and the hometown hero signed autographs for some two hours, then rode in the town's Christmas parade. He played regularly for the Rangers in 2011, hitting 16 homers in 134 games and helping Texas get back to the World Series.

All told, 20 Mississippi natives played in the major leagues in 2010 alone, a remarkable total considering the state's relatively small population and its reputation as a football haven. Among that 2010 number were emerging talents such as outfielder Julio Borbon (Starkville), left-handed pitcher Dusty Hughes (Tupelo), outfielder Seth Smith (Jackson) and left-hander Tony Sipp (Pascagoula).

If the past is prelude in baseball—and it surely is—some of these players, or some who haven't arrived in the big leagues yet, will play significant roles in the history that is yet to be written.

Spotlight

Broken Dreams

Great talent for baseball doesn't always translate into a major league career, and there can be many reasons. Kirk Presley was one of the best high school pitchers in Mississippi history, earning all kinds of awards and accolades at Tupelo High School in the early 1990s. He was 37-1 with a 0.60 ERA for his prep career. A tall right-hander—and, yes, a cousin of Elvis—Presley was drafted eighth overall in 1993 by the New York Mets.

The state held its collective breath in anticipation of how good Presley might become in professional baseball.

"There aren't many pitchers (in the Mets' system) who'll stand in his way," former Mets farm director Steve Phillips told the author. "He's certainly a priority player for us."

Presley never got out of Class A. Beset by arm injuries, he retired from baseball in 1998 at the age of 23. He pitched five pro seasons, only 147 innings all told, with 98 2/3 of those coming in his first year. His final stats: 8-10 record, 4.04 ERA.

While Presley's story is disheartening, Brian Cole's is tragic. A high school star in Meridian who broke into pro ball in the late 1990s, Cole looked to be on his way to a stellar major league career. "He was a player we were going to build around as an organization," former New York Mets general manager Dan Duquette once said.

Alas, Cole was killed in a one-car accident in Florida on March 31, 2001; he was 22. Cole was small, listed at 5 feet 9, 168 pounds, but swung a big stick. He batted .306 with 42 homers, 90 doubles, 19 triples and 193 RBIs in 320 minor league games.

He also stole 135 bases, 50 in 1999. He reached Double-A, two steps from The Show, during the 2000 season and was scheduled to start at that level in 2001. In a lawsuit against Ford Motor Company, a jury in 2010 awarded the Cole family $131 million.

Epilogue: Born to Run

Everyone in Cincinnati's Great American Ballpark knew what was about to happen.

Billy Hamilton was going to run.

It was September 3, 2013, and Hamilton, the pride of Taylorsville, was making his major league debut as a pinch runner for the Cincinnati Reds.

He had been inserted at first base in the seventh inning of a scoreless game against National League Central rival St. Louis. Yadier Molina, one of the best defensive catchers in the game, was behind the plate for the Cardinals.

No matter.

Everyone in the Great American Ballpark knew what was about to happen.

Billy Hamilton was going to run.

After all, this was the guy who had stolen 155 bases—a professional baseball record—in 2012, which he spent in A-ball and Double-A. Promoted to Triple-A for the 2013 campaign, he stole 75 bases before the Reds, contending for a playoff berth, called him up for the September stretch.

Billy Hamilton, a baseball and football star at Taylorsville High School, stole 13 bases in 14 attempts during his 2013 major league debut season
(Photo courtesy of the Cincinnati Reds)

Some called him the Reds' secret weapon—but, of course, his skill was no secret. He was put in that game on September 3 for a specific reason.

Billy Hamilton was going to run—and there he went, stealing second base and then scoring the game's only run on a subsequent single.

Hamilton would be successful on his first 13 stolen base tries for the Reds before finally getting thrown out in his last attempt of the season.

Perhaps baseball witnessed the birth of star that month, though those things are impossible to predict. Just the fact that Billy Hamilton had reached the major leagues was a surprise to some.

~ ~ ~

Research for this book had to stop somewhere, and it stopped following the 2011 season. Baseball, of course, marches on, and over the next two seasons, a new batch of Mississippians arrived on the big league stage. Joining Hamilton in this group were Brandon's Tyler Moore, Tupelo native Brian Dozier, Robert Carson from Hattiesburg and Meridian's Corey Dickerson.

Watching their development is among the many things that draw us to the game. Others will follow, all gifted in some rare way, all hoping to make a mark in baseball where many have tried and failed.

How Hamilton's career might evolve is intriguing, to say the least. He has something special, a gift those in baseball call a plus-plus tool. The baseball scouts who flocked to see him play at Taylorsville High School several years ago didn't have to watch for long to see it.

"Billy is the fastest thing I've ever seen on a baseball field – and I've been doing this a long time," said a Mississippi-based scout who works for a National League team.

Hamilton was also a football star at Taylorsville, good enough as a wide receiver to receive a scholarship to play at Mississippi State. There were some who argued that his best sport might be basketball, that he could be the second coming of onetime NBA star Allen Iverson.

Sports just came easy to Hamilton in high school.

But there are questions that pro baseball scouts have about virtually every high school phenom: Does he have the makeup to survive in the pro game, where everybody was a high school star? Is he willing to put in the work, which can take several years, to make it to the major leagues?

"I didn't have any doubts," said the National League scout, whose organization liked Hamilton but didn't draft him. "In a small town like Taylorsville, you can get information on kids pretty easy. Nobody in Taylorsville said a bad thing about Billy. I'm telling you, if he had any baggage in his past, we'd have heard about it."

Some major league teams assumed Hamilton was more interested in playing football at State than riding the buses in the minor leagues. Some, but not all.

"You could see in the way he played the game that he loved baseball," the National League scout said. "And he told me straight up, 'I want to be a big leaguer.' Now, he wanted to be drafted in a high round, but he was about more than the money. He told me, 'I want to make something of myself.'"

The Cincinnati Reds drafted the 6-foot-1, 150-pound Hamilton in the second round of the 2009 amateur draft and signed him for a $623,000 bonus.

Within a couple of years, he had made himself into one of the most exciting players in the minor leagues. "When he arrives in the big leagues," Baseball America editors wrote in the 2013 *Prospect Handbook*, "he'll spur ticket sales with his style of play."

Hamilton started slowly in pro ball, as many figured he would, considering the level of competition he faced at a small high school.

"He could make the spectacular play without even thinking about it," the National League scout said. "What he needed work on was the fundamental stuff, just learning the routines of pro ball."

Hamilton, a switch-hitter, batted just .205 in the rookie Gulf Coast League in the summer of 2009, though he did steal 14 bases in 43 games. Hamilton made great strides as a hitter the next year, at Billings in the rookie Pioneer League. He hit .318, rapped out 10 triples and stole 48 bags in 69 games.

Facing better competition at low Class A Dayton in the Midwest League in 2011, Hamilton hit .278 and stole 103 bases in 135 games. If there was a concern at that time, it was his high strikeout total (133).

The Reds promoted Hamilton again in 2012, sending him to the high-A California League, and he answered the challenge. In 82 games for Bakersfield, he hit .278 and improved his plate discipline (70 strikeouts/50 walks).

He also captured the fancy of the baseball nation with his base-stealing exploits. He had 104 when the Reds moved him up to Double-A Pensacola in July of that year. Double-A is regarded as the biggest jump a player has to make in the minor leagues. Hamilton cleared the hurdle with ease, batting .286 in 50 games with the Pelicans while stealing 51 more bases to set the professional single-season record of 155.

Scouts who followed him closely at Taylorsville probably weren't surprised that Hamilton pulled off such a feat.

"Every time you'd go see him play, he'd do something that made you say, 'No way,'" said the National League scout. "He was electrifying. ... He didn't hit the ball hard, but he could make things happen. He had great instincts for the game. And as fast as he was, he was also cheetah quick. On the bases, he was almost impossible to throw out."

Hamilton, who moved from shortstop to center field at Triple-A Louisville in 2013, was invited for the second straight year to play in the prestigious All-Star Futures Game that summer. He was hitting .256 at Louisville when the Reds called him up on Sept. 2 and he had adjusted well to center field, where, Baseball

America says, he projects in the major leagues as a plus-defender and a potential Gold Glove winner.

"I'm not surprised by how well he's done," the scout said before Hamilton's promotion. "He's swinging (the bat) better than I thought he would at this point in his career. I'm a little surprised at how fast he's developed. The Reds have done a great job with him. They've let Billy be Billy and use his strengths.

"I root for Billy. People in Mississippi should root for him … we should be proud of him."

The Players

From Baseball Almanac
(From 1901 through the 2011 season)

**Player's name, Place of Birth (Date of Birth/year-
month-day) Debut Year**
Career capsule
*Active in 2011

Al Baker, Batesville (1906-02-28) 1938
Right-hander appeared in three games with the Boston
Red Sox.

Frank Baker, Meridian (1946-10-29) 1970
Second baseman/shortstop, a Southern Miss alumnus,
batted .191 in 146 games over four seasons with the
New York Yankees and Baltimore.

Frank Barnes, Longwood (1926-08-26) 1957
Right-hander appeared in six games over three seasons
with the St. Louis Cardinals and posted an 0-2 record
with one save.

Norm Bass, Laurel (1939-01-21) 1961
Right-hander, who overcame meningitis as a child, went
13-17 with a 5.31 ERA in 65 games over three seasons
with the Kansas City Athletics. Also played one game
with Denver in the American Football League in 1964.

Howard Battle, Biloxi (1972-03-25) 1995
Third baseman batted .243 with one home run in 29
games over three seasons with three teams: Toronto,
Philadelphia and Atlanta. Drafted out of Mercy Cross
High by the Blue Jays in the fourth round in 1990.

Jim Bivin, Jackson (1909-12-11) 1935
Right-hander appeared in 47 games in one season with
the Philadelphia Phillies and was 2-9 with a 5.78 ERA.

Buddy Blair, Columbia (1910-09-10) 1942
Left-handed hitting third baseman played one year for
the Philadelphia A's, batting .279 with five homers and
66 RBIs. Served in the Air Force in World War II, then
became a minor league manager. Starred in track and
basketball at LSU.

Don Blasingame, Corinth (1932-03-16) 1955
Left-handed hitting second baseman played in 1,444
games with five teams over 12 seasons, batting .258.
Was an All-Star in 1958 with the St. Louis Cardinals, his
original team. Nicknamed "The Corinth Comet."

Milt Bolling, Mississippi City (1930-08-09) 1952
Infielder played in 400 games with three teams (Boston
Red Sox, Washington Senators and Detroit) over seven
seasons, batting .241. Spent most of his playing career
with the Red Sox and later worked in the team's front
office and as a scout.

Glen Bolton, Booneville (1904-02-13) 1928
Left-handed hitting first baseman, a Mississippi State
alumnus, played four games for the Cleveland Indians in
his only season.

Josh Booty, Starkville (1975-04-29) 1996
Third baseman, better known as an LSU quarterback,
played 13 games over three seasons with Florida.
Drafted in the first round out of a Louisiana high school
in 1994.

*Julio Borbon, Starkville (1986-02-20) 2009

Left-handed hitting outfielder batted .282 in 215 games over three seasons with Texas. Played regularly in center field in 2010 and hit .276 with 42 RBIs, 60 runs and 15 steals.

Bob Boyd, Potts Camp (1919-10-01) 1951
Lefty-hitting first baseman/outfielder batted .293 in 693 games with four teams: Chicago White Sox, Baltimore, Kansas City A's and Milwaukee Braves. Hit .318 as a regular for Baltimore in 1957. Started his pro career in the Negro Leagues, debuting in the majors at age 31. Nicknamed "The Rope."

Dennis "Oil Can" Boyd, Meridian (1959-10-06) 1982
Right-hander, a Jackson State product, notched a 78-77 record with a 4.04 ERA in 10 seasons with three teams, Boston, Montreal and Texas. Won 16 games for the 1986 Boston Red Sox, who lost to the New York Mets in seven games in the World Series.

Chad Bradford, Jackson (1974-09-14) 1998
Submarine-style right-hander, who retired in 2009, won 36 games and saved 11 with a 3.26 ERA in 561 appearances, all in relief. Posted a 0.39 ERA in 24 postseason games. Pitched for six different teams. Featured prominently in the book and movie "Moneyball."

Jeff Branson, Waynesboro (1967-01-26) 1992
Left-handed hitting infielder batted .246 over nine seasons with three teams. Hit .260 with 12 home runs for the 1995 Cincinnati Reds. Appeared in the 1997 World Series with Cleveland. Finished his career with the Los Angeles Dodgers.

Marshall Bridges, Jackson (1931-06-02) 1959

Left-hander was 23-15 with 25 saves and a 3.75 ERA over seven years with four teams, St. Louis Cardinals, Cincinnati, New York Yankees and Washington Senators. Won eight games and saved 18 for the pennant-winning Yankees in 1962. Nicknamed "Sheriff."

Adrian Brown, McComb (1974-02-07) 1997
Switch-hitting outfielder batted .258 over nine seasons with four teams: Pittsburgh, Boston, Kansas City and Texas. Hit .315 with 13 steals and 64 runs in 104 games for Pittsburgh in 2000. Drafted in the 48th round out of McComb High by the Pirates in 1992.

Chris Brown, Jackson (1961-08-15) 1984
Third baseman hit .269 with 38 home runs in 449 games over six seasons with three teams, San Francisco, San Diego and Detroit. Made the All-Star Game in 1986, when he hit .317 for the Giants. Died under mysterious circumstances in 2006.

Jake Brown, Sumrall (1948-03-22) 1975
Outfielder got 43 at-bats for San Francisco in his lone season, batting .209. No. 2 overall draft pick out of Southern (La.) University by the Giants in 1969.

Jamie Brown, Meridian (1977-03-31) 2004
Right-hander made four appearances for Boston in his only season, posting a 5.87 ERA. Originally drafted by Cleveland in 1996.

Roosevelt Brown, Vicksburg (1975-08-03) 1999
Left-handed hitting outfielder played four seasons with the Chicago Cubs, batting .251 with 11 homers. Hit .352 in 98 at-bats in 2000.

Red Bullock, Biloxi (1911-10-12) 1936
Left-handed pitcher, a Millsaps College alumnus, went
0-2 with a 14.04 ERA in 12 games in one season with
the Philadelphia A's.

Ellis Burks, Vicksburg (1964-09-11) 1987
Outfielder, a two-time All-Star, played 18 years with
five different teams and batted .291 with 352 home runs
and 1,206 RBIs. First-round draft pick out of a Texas
junior college by Boston in 1983. Had a 20-homer/20-
steal season as a Red Sox rookie in 1987. Hit .344 with
40 homers and 128 RBIs for Colorado in 1996, finishing
third in the National League MVP voting.

Paul Busby, Waynesboro (1918-08-25) 1941
Left-handed hitting outfielder batted .268 in 36 games
over two seasons with the Philadelphia Phillies. Served
in the Army in World War II.

Guy Bush, Aberdeen (1901-08-23) 1923
Right-hander went 176-136 with a 3.86 ERA in a 17-
year career with five different clubs. Spent his first 12
seasons with the Chicago Cubs, winning 152 games (20
in 1933, 19 in '32 and 18 twice). Appeared in two World
Series for the Cubs. Managed in the All-American Girls
Professional Baseball League.

Sol Carter, Picayune (1908-12-23) 1931
Right-hander appeared in two games for the 1931
Philadelphia A's. Allowed a hit, four walks and five
runs.

Calvin Chapman, Courtland (1910-12-20) 1935

Left-handed hitting outfielder/second baseman played 111 games in two years with Cincinnati. Batted .265 with one home run.

Ed Chapman, Courtland (1905-11-28) 1933
Right-hander, a Mississippi State product, made six appearances (8.00 ERA) for the Washington Senators in his only season. Brother of Calvin Chapman.

Danny Clark, Meridian (1894-01-18) 1922
Left-handed hitting infielder played 245 games in three seasons, one each with Detroit, Boston Red Sox and St. Louis Cardinals. Batted .277 with eight triples and five homers.

Dave Clark, Tupelo (1962-09-03) 1986
Left-handed hitting outfielder, a Jackson State alum, played 13 years with six teams. Batted .264 with 62 homers and 284 RBIs. Drafted in the first round by Cleveland in 1993. Served as interim manager of the Houston Astros, for whom he played one season, in 2009.

Stan Cliburn, Jackson (1956-12-19) 1980
Catcher appeared in 54 games (56 at-bats) for the California Angels in his lone season. Batted .179 with two homers.

Stewart Cliburn, Jackson (1956-12-19) 1984
Right-hander, a Delta State product, made 85 appearances in three seasons with the California Angels. Posted a 13-5 record with six saves and a 4.07 ERA. Twin brother of Stan Cliburn.

*Louis Coleman, Greenwood (1986-04-04) 2011

Right-hander, a Pillow Academy graduate who starred at LSU, posted a 2.87 ERA with a 1-4 record and one save in 48 relief appearances for Kansas City.

Billy Cowan, Calhoun City (1938-08-28) 1963
Outfielder/first baseman played for eight years with six different teams. Batted .236 with 40 home runs and 125 RBIs in 493 games. Played regularly for the Chicago Cubs in 1964, batting .241 with 19 homers and 50 RBIs.

Harry Craft, Ellisville (1915-04-19) 1937
Center fielder, a Mississippi College alum, played six seasons with Cincinnati, including pennant-winning teams in 1939 and '40. Batted .253 with 44 homers and 267 RBIs. Twice led National League center fielders in putouts. Served in the Navy in World War II. Managed the Kansas City A's and Houston Colt .45s. Nicknamed "Popeye."

Dode Criss, Sherman (1885-03-12) 1908
Right-handed pitcher and left-handed hitting outfielder/first baseman played four seasons with the St. Louis Browns. Batted .276 in 227 games. Went 3-9 with a 4.38 ERA in 30 pitching appearances.

Hughie Critz, Starkville (1900-09-17) 1924
Second baseman, a Mississippi State product, hit .268 with 38 homers, 531 RBIs and 97 stolen bases in 12 years with two teams, Cincinnati and the New York Giants. Second in National League MVP voting in 1926 (.270, 79 RBIs, 96 runs for the Reds).

*Dewon Day, Jackson (1980-09-29) 2007

Right-hander, a Jackson State alum, made 13 appearances for the Chicago White Sox in his one season, posting an 11.25 ERA. Originally drafted by Toronto.

Tommy Dean, Iuka (1945-08-30) 1967
Shortstop/third baseman batted .180 in 215 games over four seasons with the Los Angeles Dodgers and San Diego. Got 273 at-bats with the expansion Padres in 1969 and batted .176.

Bob Didier, Hattiesburg (1949-02-16) 1969
Switch-hitting catcher played six years with three clubs: Atlanta, Detroit and Boston. Batted .229 without a home run in 247 games. Hit .256 in 114 games as a rookie regular for the Braves in 1969.

Atley Donald, Morton (1910-08-19) 1938
Right-hander posted a 65-33 record with a 3.52 ERA in eight seasons with the New York Yankees. Twice won 13 games in a season. Pitched in two World Series, 1941 and '42.

Matt Duff, Clarksdale (1974-10-06) 2002
Right-hander, an Ole Miss product, made seven appearances (4.76 ERA) for St. Louis in his lone season.

*Jarrod Dyson, McComb (1984-08-15) 2010
Left-handed hitting center fielder batted .208 in 34 games for Kansas City in 2010 and '11. Stole 20 bases in 22 attempts. Drafted in the 50th (and final) round by the Royals from Southwest Mississippi Community College in 2006.

Luke Easter, Jonestown (1915-08-04) 1949

Left-handed hitting first baseman/outfielder hit .274 with 93 homers and 340 RBIs in six seasons with the Cleveland Indians. First black Mississippi native to play in the major leagues. Was 34 when he made his debut. Starred in the Negro Leagues before signing with the Indians and played minor league ball until age 49.

Jim Joe Edwards, Banner (1894-12-14) 1922
Left-hander, a Mississippi College alum, pitched six seasons with three teams, the Cleveland Indians, Chicago White Sox and Cincinnati. Posted a 26-37 record with a 4.37 ERA. Won 10 games for the 1923 Indians. Nicknamed "Little Joe" though he stood 6 feet 2.

Bobby Etheridge, Greenville (1942-11-25) 1967
Third baseman, a Mississippi State alumnus, played two years for San Francisco, hitting .244 in 96 games.

Joe "Doc" Evans, Meridian (1895-05-15) 1915
Outfielder/third baseman, an Ole Miss product, played 11 years with three teams, the Cleveland Indians, St. Louis Browns and Washington. Batted .259 with 31 triples and 67 steals. Spent eight seasons with the Indians and hit .308 in their 1920 World Series victory.

Dave "Boo" Ferriss, Shaw (1921-12-05) 1945
Right-hander, a Mississippi State alum, went 65-30 with a 3.65 ERA over six years in an injury-curtailed career with the Boston Red Sox. Went 21-10 as a rookie in 1945 and 25-6 for the '46 pennant-winning club. Won a game in the World Series against St. Louis. Won 639 games in a 29-year coaching career at Delta State.

Curtis Ford, Jackson (1960-10-11) 1985

Left-hander hitting outfielder, a Jackson State product, played 406 games over six years with St. Louis and Philadelphia. Batted .245 with 36 stolen bases. Went 4-for-14 in the 1987 World Series with the Cardinals.

Art Gardner, Madden (1952-09-21) 1975
Left-handed hitting outfielder played in 86 games over three seasons with Houston and San Francisco, batting .162. Drafted in the second round by the Astros in 1971 out of South Leake High. Later worked for the Major League Scouting Bureau.

Joey Gathright, Hattiesburg (1981-04-27) 2004
Left-handed hitting center fielder batted .263 with 81 stolen bases in 452 games over seven seasons with four clubs. Drafted out of a Louisiana high school by Tampa Bay. Hit .307 in 74 games for Kansas City in 2007.

Joe Gibbon, Hickory (1935-04-10) 1960
Left-hander, a baseball and basketball star at Ole Miss, played 13 years with four teams, going 61-65 with a 3.52 ERA. Played eight years for Pittsburgh, appearing in the 1960 World Series (won by the Pirates over the New York Yankees in seven games) and winning 13 games in 1961.

Jake Gibbs, Grenada (1938-11-07) 1962
Left-handed hitting catcher, a baseball and football standout at Ole Miss, played 10 seasons for the New York Yankees, batting .233 with 25 homers and 146 RBIs. Batted .301 with eight homers in 49 games in 1970, his next-to-last season. Coached for 19 years at Ole Miss.

Rod Gilbreath, Laurel (1952-09-24) 1972

213

Second baseman/third baseman played 500 games over seven years, all with Atlanta. Batted .248 with 14 home runs and 125 RBIs. In 128 games in 1977, hit .243 with eight homers and 43 RBIs.

George Gill, Catchings (1909-02-13) 1937
Right-hander, a Mississippi College alumnus, went 24-26 with a 5.05 ERA over three seasons. Was 11-4 with a 4.51 as a rookie for Detroit, then went 12-9, 4.12 in 1938. Traded to the St. Louis Browns in 1939.

Lorenzo Gray, Mound Bayou (1958-03-04) 1982
Third baseman played 58 games in two seasons with the Chicago White Sox. Batted .208 with one home run.

Paul Gregory, Tomnolen (1908-06-09) 1932
Right-hander, a Mississippi State product, was 9-14 with a 4.72 ERA in two years with the Chicago White Sox. Served in the Navy during World War II. Coached 21 years at his alma mater.

Luther Hackman, Columbus (1974-10-10) 1999
Right-hander posted a 9-10 record with a 5.09 ERA over five seasons with three teams: Colorado, St. Louis and San Diego. Went 5-4, 4.11 in 43 games for the Cardinals in 2002.

Sam Hairston, Crawford (1920-01-20) 1951
Catcher, a Negro Leagues star for many years, went 2-for-5 in four games for the Chicago White Sox. Had two sons and two grandsons play in the majors.

*Bill Hall, Nettleton (1979-12-28) 2002
Infielder/outfielder played 10 years with five different teams. Batted .249 with 124 homers and 439 RBIs.

214

Spent his first eight years with Milwaukee and hit .270 with 35 homers, 85 RBIs and 39 doubles in 2006.

Josh Hancock, Cleveland (1978-04-11) 2002
Right-hander went 9-7 with a 4.20 ERA over six seasons with four teams: Boston, Philadelphia, Cincinnati and St. Louis. Posted a 4.09 ERA in 62 games for St. Louis in 2006 and was on the World Series roster but did not pitch during the Cardinals' victory. Died in a car wreck on April 29, 2007, while with the Cardinals.

Mickey Harrington, Hattiesburg (1934-10-08) 1963
Outfielder/first baseman, a Southern Miss alum, made one pinch-running appearance for Philadelphia. Played 1,091 minor league games and batted .290 with 80 homers.

Charlie Hayes, Hattiesburg (1965-05-29) 1988
Third baseman/first baseman played 14 seasons with seven teams, batting .262 with 144 home runs and 740 RBIs. Hit .305 with 25 homers, 98 RBIs and 45 doubles for Colorado's inaugural team in 1993. Won a World Series ring with the New York Yankees in 1996. Also played in the Little League World Series.

Joe Henderson, Lake Cormorant (1946-07-04) 1974
Right-hander went 3-2 with a 6.69 ERA over three seasons (16 games) with Cincinnati and the Chicago White Sox. Posted a 0.00 ERA in 11 innings for the 1976 Reds championship team but didn't pitch in the postseason.

Larry Herndon, Sunflower (1953-11-03) 1974
Right-handed hitting outfielder batted .270 with 107 home runs, 550 RBIs and 76 triples in 14 seasons (1,537 games) with three teams: St. Louis, San Francisco and

Detroit. Batted .280 for the 1984 Tigers and hit .333 during their World Series victory.

George Hockette, Perth (1908-04-07) 1934
Left-hander pitched for two seasons with the Boston Red Sox, going 4-4 with a 4.08 ERA in 26 appearances.

*Jarrett Hoffpauir, Natchez (1983-06-18) 2009
Second baseman/third baseman, a Southern Miss alum, batted .217 in 21 games over two seasons, playing for St. Louis and Toronto.

Sammy Holbrook, Meridian (1910-07-17) 1935
Catcher played 52 games for Washington in his lone season, batting .259 with two homers and 25 RBIs.

Don Hopkins, West Point (1952-01-09) 1975
Outfielder/pinch runner appeared in 82 games for Oakland in 1975, stealing 21 bases in 30 attempts. Batted just six times (one hit). Played three games for the A's in '76.

Dave Hoskins, Greenwood (1925-08-03) 1953
Right-hander posted a 9-4 record with a 3.81 ERA in two seasons with Cleveland. Went 9-3, 3.99 in 26 games (and batted .259 with a homer and nine RBIs) for the '53 Indians. Played three years in the Negro Leagues.

Jim Howarth, Biloxi (1947-03-07) 1971
Left-handed hitting outfielder, a Mississippi State product, batted .217 over four seasons with San Francisco. Hit .235 with a homer and seven RBIs in 119 at-bats in 1972.

*Dusty Hughes, Tupelo (1982-06-29) 2009

Left-hander, a Delta State alumnus, made 80 appearances over three years with Kansas City and Minnesota, going 2-5 with a 4.99 ERA. Posted a 3.83 in 57 games with the Royals in 2010.

*Rhyne Hughes, Picayune (1983-09-09) 2010
Left-handed hitting first baseman, a Pearl River Community College product, batted .213 in 14 games in his one season with Baltimore.

Cleo James, Clarksdale (1940-08-31) 1968
Outfielder batted .228 with five homers and 27 RBIs over four years (208 games) with the Los Angeles Dodgers and Chicago Cubs. Batted .287 with two homers and 13 RBIs in 150 at-bats for the Cubs in 1971.

Al Jones, Charleston (1959-02-10) 1983
Right-hander, an Alcorn State alum, was 2-1 with a 3.77 ERA and five saves in 27 games over three seasons with the Chicago White Sox.

Dalton Jones, McComb (1943-12-10) 1964
Left-handed hitting second baseman/third baseman played 907 games over nine seasons with Boston and Detroit. Batted .235 with 41 homers and 237 RBIs. Hit .289 for the 1967 Red Sox and .389 in the World Series that year. Compiled 55 career pinch hits, still a Boston record through 2011.

Dick Jones, Meadville (1902-05-22) 1926
Right-hander went 2-1 with a 6.66 ERA in six games over two years with Washington.

Ricky Jones, Tupelo (1958-06-04) 1986
Infielder batted .182 in 16 games for Baltimore in his only season.

Benn Karr, Mount Pleasant (1893-11-28) 1920
Right-hander posted a 35-48 record with a 4.60 ERA
over six years with the Boston Red Sox and Cleveland.
Won 11 games for the Indians in 1925. Nicknamed
"Baldy."

Jack Knight, Pittsboro (1895-01-12) 1922
Right-hander, a Millsaps College alumnus, went 10-18
with a 6.85 ERA in 72 games over four years with three
National League clubs: St. Louis, Philadelphia and
Boston.

Gene Lambert, Crenshaw (1921-04-26) 1941
Right-hander pitched in three games over two years with
the Philadelphia Phillies, going 0-1 with a 2.70 ERA.

Doc Land, Binnsville (1903-05-14) 1929
Left-handed hitting outfielder went 0-for-3 with a walk
in his one game for Washington. Given name William
Gilbert.

Marcus Lawton, Gulfport (1965-08-18) 1989
Switch-hitting outfielder batted .214 in 10 games for the
New York Yankees in his lone season. Drafted in the
sixth round by the New York Mets in 1983. Stole 111
bases in the minors in 1985. Had one major league steal.

Matt Lawton, Gulfport (1971-11-30) 1995
Left-handed hitting outfielder, a Mississippi Gulf Coast
Community College alum, played 12 years with seven
teams, batting .267 with 138 home runs, 631 RBIs and
165 stolen bases. Hit .305 with 13 homers, 88 RBIs and
23 steals in 2000 with Minnesota, where he played seven
years. A two-time All-Star. Brother of Marcus Lawton.

*Brent Leach, Flowood (1982-11-18) 2009
Left-hander, a Southern Miss and Delta State alum,
posted a 5.75 ERA in 38 games with the Los Angeles
Dodgers.

Hal Lee, Ludlow (1905-02-15) 1930
Outfielder, a Mississippi College product, played seven
years with three National League clubs (Brooklyn,
Philadelphia and Boston) and hit .275 with 33 homers
and 323 RBIs. Belted 18 homers in 149 games for the
Phillies in 1932.

Chet Lemon, Jackson (1955-02-12) 1975
Outfielder batted .273 with 215 home runs and 884 RBIs
over 16 seasons with the Chicago White Sox and Detroit
Tigers. Three-time All-Star. Set an American League
record with 512 putouts in 1977 with the ChiSox. Four
times led the league in being hit by a pitch. Won a
World Series ring with the Tigers in 1984.

Sam Leslie, Moss Point (1905-07-26) 1929
Left-handed hitting first baseman batted .304 over 10
seasons (822 games) with two National League teams,
New York and Brooklyn. Hit .332 with 102 RBIs for
1934 Dodgers. Played in the 1936 and '37 World Series
with the Giants.

*Fred Lewis, Hattiesburg (1980-12-09) 2006
Left-handed hitting outfielder, a Mississippi Gulf Coast
Community College product, batted .267 with 27
homers, 136 RBIs and 53 steals over six years with San
Francisco, Toronto and Cincinnati. Hit .282 with nine
homers and 21 steals in 2008 for the Giants, who drafted
him in the second round out of Southern (La.) University
in 2002.

*John Lindsey, Hattiesburg (1977-01-30) 2010
First baseman went 1-for-12 in his lone season with the
Los Angeles Dodgers. Spent 16 years in the minors
before getting the major league call-up.

Nook Logan, Natchez (1979-11-28) 2004
Switch-hitting outfielder, a Copiah-Lincoln Community
College alumnus, hit .268 with 56 stolen bases in four
seasons with two teams, Detroit and Washington. Stole
23 bases in both the 2005 (Tigers) and 2007 (Nationals)
seasons.

Slim Love, Love (1890-08-01) 1913
Left-hander posted a 28-21 record with a 3.04 ERA in
six seasons with three American League clubs,
Washington, New York and Detroit. Went 13-12, 3.07
for the 1918 Yankees. Stood 6 feet 7. Given name
Edward Haughton.

Jim Lyle, Lake (1900-07-24) 1925
Right-hander, a Mississippi State alum, pitched three
innings (two runs) for Washington in his lone season.

Barry Lyons, Biloxi (1960-06-03) 1986
Catcher, a Delta State product, batted .239 with 15
homers and 89 RBIs over seven years (253 games) with
four teams: the New York Mets, Los Angeles Dodgers,
California and the Chicago White Sox. Hit .266 with
five homers in 27 games for the 2005 White Sox.

Dave Madison, Brooksville (1921-02-01) 1950
Right-hander pitched three seasons, posting an 8-7 mark
with a 5.70 ERA. Played for the New York Yankees, St.
Louis Browns and Detroit.

Wendell Magee, Hattiesburg (1972-08-03) 1996

Outfielder hit .247 with 24 home runs and 122 RBIs over seven seasons (386 games) with Philadelphia and Detroit. Batted .271 with six homers and 35 RBIs with the Tigers in 2002, his last major league season.

*Paul Maholm, Greenwood (1982-06-25) 2005
Left-hander, a Mississippi State product, posted a 53-73 record and a 4.36 ERA in seven years with Pittsburgh. Drafted in the first round (eighth overall) in 2003.

Doc Marshall, New Albany (1906-06-04) 1929
Infielder, an Ole Miss alumnus, played four seasons (219 games) with the New York Giants, batting .258 with no home runs and 61 RBIs.

Brian Maxcy, Amory (1971-05-04) 1995
Right-hander, an Ole Miss product, went 4-5 with a 7.28 ERA in two years with Detroit. Made 41 of his 43 career appearances in 1995.

Lewis "Sport" McAllister, Austin (1874-07-23) 1896
Switch-hitter who threw right-handed played every position over a seven-year career with three clubs. Batted .247 with 164 RBIs in 418 games. Posted a 4-7 record with a 5.32 ERA in 17 games as a pitcher.

Bob McCrory, Steens (1982-05-03) 2008
Right-hander, a Southern Miss alumnus, put up a 16.46 ERA in 15 games over two seasons with Baltimore. Drafted in the fourth round in 2003.

Allen McDill, Greenville (1971-08-23) 1997
Left-hander made 38 appearances over four seasons for three clubs (Kansas City, Boston and Detroit) and had a 7.79 ERA.

Pat McGehee, Meadville (1888-07-02) 1912
Right-hander made one start (one hit, one walk, no outs recorded) for Detroit.

Eric McNair, Meridian (1909-04-12) 1929
Infielder batted .274 with 82 home runs and 633 RBIs over a 14-year career with four American League clubs, Philadelphia, Boston, Detroit and Chicago. Batted .285 with 18 homers, 95 RBIs and a league-best 47 doubles with the 1932 A's. Played in two World Series with Philly. Nicknamed "Boob."

Bill Melton, Gulfport (1945-07-07) 1968
Third baseman/outfielder hit .253 with 160 homers and 591 RBIs in a 10-year career with three American League teams, Chicago, California and Cleveland. Led the AL in homers in 1971 with 33 for the White Sox, for whom he played eight seasons. Made one All-Star Game.

John Howard "Lefty" Merritt, Plantersville/Tupelo (1894-10-12) 1913
Outfielder, who won 215 games as a pitcher in the minors, got into one game (no at-bats) for the New York Giants.

Jim Miles, Grenada (1943-08-08) 1968
Right-hander, a Delta State alumnus, posted a 7.30 ERA in 13 games over two seasons with Washington. Coached for 22 years at Northwest Mississippi Community College, where he also played.

Mike Miley, Yazoo City (1953-03-30) 1975
Switching-hitting shortstop played 84 games in two years with California, batting .176. First-round draft pick

out of LSU, where he also played quarterback, in 1974. Died in a car accident on Jan. 6, 1977.

Matt Miller, Greenwood (1971-11-23) 2003
Right-hander, a Delta State alumnus, went 6-1 with a 2.72 ERA in 100 relief appearances over five years with Colorado and Cleveland. Notched only two career saves.

Monroe Mitchell, Starkville (1901-09-11) 1923
Right-hander, who played at Mississippi State, went 2-4 with a 6.48 ERA in 10 games in one season with the Washington Senators.

Willie Mitchell, Pleasant Grove (1889-12-01) 1909
Left-hander, a Mississippi State product, posted a 2.88 ERA and an 83-92 record in 276 games over 11 seasons with two clubs, Cleveland and Detroit. Went 14-8 with a 1.91 ERA for the 1913 Indians.

Wilmer "Vinegar Bend" Mizell, Leakesville (1930-08-13) 1952
Left-hander won 90 games (88 losses) with a 3.85 ERA over an 11-season career with three National League clubs, St. Louis, Pittsburgh and the New York Mets. Made two All-Star teams and pitched in the 1960 World Series for the champion Pirates. Served three terms as a North Carolina congressman. Nickname came from a town in Alabama where he played ball as an amateur.

Dustan Mohr, Hattiesburg (1976-06-19) 2001
Outfielder played for five different teams over seven seasons, batting .249 with 49 homers and 156 RBIs. Hit .269 with 12 homers in 120 games for Minnesota in 2002 and belted 17 homers for Colorado in 2005.

*Mitch Moreland, Amory (1985-09-06) 2010

Left-handed hitting first baseman/outfielder, a Mississippi State alumnus, played two seasons with Texas, batting .258 with 25 home runs and 76 RBIs. Went 7-for-23 with two homers in the 2010 and '11 World Series.

Chet Morgan, Cleveland/Skene (1910-06-06) 1935
Left-handed hitting outfielder played in 88 games over two seasons with Detroit, batting .277.

Jerry Moses, Yazoo City (1946-08-09) 1965
Catcher batted .251 with 25 home runs and 109 RBIs in 386 games over nine years with seven clubs. Hit .263 with six homers and 35 RBIs in 92 games for the 1970 Boston Red Sox.

Charlie Moss, Meridian (1911-03-20) 1934
Catcher, an Ole Miss alumnus, played parts of three seasons with the Philadelphia A's, batting .246 in 47 games.

Buddy Myer, Ellisville (1904-03-16) 1925
Left-handed hitting second baseman/shortstop, a Mississippi State product, batted .303 over a 17-year career. Made two All-Star teams. Won the American League batting title in 1935 with a .349 average for Washington, with which he spent 16 years. Stole a league-high 30 bases for the Boston Red Sox in 1928. Stole 157 bases all told and drove in 848 runs.

Bobby Myrick, Hattiesburg (1952-10-01) 1976
Left-hander, a Mississippi State alumnus, posted a 3.48 ERA in 82 games over three years with the New York Mets. Great nephew of Buddy Myer.

Dolan Nichols, Tishomingo (1930-02-28) 1958

Right-hander made 24 appearances in his one year with the Chicago Cubs, going 0-4 with a 5.01 ERA.

Leo Norris, Bay St. Louis (1908-05-17) 1936
Infielder batted .262 with 20 home runs and 112 RBIs in two seasons with the Philadelphia Phillies.

Ryan Nye, Biloxi (1973-06-24) 1997
Right-hander went 0-2 with a 9.69 ERA in five games over two years with Philadelphia.

*Roy Oswalt, Kosciusko (1977-08-29) 2001
Right-hander, a Holmes Community College product, was 154-92 with a 3.21 ERA over 12 seasons with Houston and Philadelphia. Twice won 20 games for the Astros. Was a three-time All-Star. Had a 5-2 postseason record and pitched in the 2005 World Series for Houston.

Dave Parker, Calhoun City (1951-06-09) 1973
Left-handed hitting outfielder/DH played 19 seasons with six teams, batting .290 with 339 home runs, 1,493 RBIs and 2,712 hits. Earned National League MVP honors in 1978 with Pittsburgh, where he spent 11 years. Won two World Series rings ('79 Pittsburgh, '89 Oakland), made seven All-Star teams and picked up three Gold Gloves. Nicknamed "Cobra."

Claude Passeau, Waynesboro (1909-04-09) 1935
Right-hander, a Millsaps College alumnus, posted a 162-150 record with a 3.32 ERA over a 13-year career with three National League clubs: Chicago (nine seasons), Philadelphia and Pittsburgh. Made five All-Star teams. Won a game for the Cubs in the 1945 World Series.

Ike Pearson, Grenada (1917-03-01) 1939
Right-hander, an Ole Miss product, went 13-50 with a
4.83 ERA in six years, five with the Philadelphia Phillies
and one with the Chicago White Sox. Served in the
Marine Corps during World War II.

Steve Pegues, Pontotoc (1968-05-21) 1994
Outfielder, a first-round pick by Detroit in 1987, batted
.266 in 100 career games with Cincinnati and Pittsburgh.
Hit all of his six career homers in 1995 for the Pirates.

Hugh Laurin Pepper, Vaughan (1931-01-18) 1954
Right-hander, a baseball and football standout at
Southern Miss, made 44 appearances over four seasons
with Pittsburgh, going 2-8 with a 7.06 ERA.

Bubba Phillips, West Point (1928-02-24) 1955
Third baseman/outfielder, a baseball and football player
at Southern Miss, hit .255 with 62 homers and 356 RBIs
over 10 seasons with three American League teams:
Detroit, Chicago and Cleveland. Played in the 1959
World Series for the White Sox. Batted .264 with 18
homers and 72 RBIs for the Indians in 1961.

Jack Pierce, Laurel (1948-06-02) 1973
Left-handed hitting first baseman batted .211 in 70
games over three years with Atlanta and Detroit. Totaled
eight home runs and 22 RBIs in 53 games for the Tigers
in 1975.

Jay Powell, Meridian (1972-01-09) 1995
Right-hander, a Mississippi State alum, put up a 4.17
ERA with a 36-23 record and 22 saves over 11 seasons
with five clubs. Won Game 7 of the 1997 World Series
for Florida. Drafted in the first round in 1993 by
Baltimore.

Jackie Price, Winborn (1912-11-13) 1946
Left-handed hitting shortstop went 3-for-13 (.231) in
seven games in his one year with the Cleveland Indians.

Frank Ragland, Water Valley (1904-05-26) 1932
Right-hander went 1-4 with a 7.11 ERA in 23 games
over two seasons with Washington and the Philadelphia
Phillies.

Gary Rath, Gulfport (1973-01-10) 1998
Left-hander, a Mississippi State product, had a 11.25
ERA in eight games over two years with Minnesota and
the Los Angeles Dodgers. Became head coach at
Mississippi Gulf Coast Community College in 2010.

Phil Redding, Crystal Springs (1889-12-08) 1912
Right-hander went 2-1 with a 5.14 ERA in four games
over two seasons with the St. Louis Cardinals.

Jack Reed, Silver City (1933-02-02) 1961
Outfielder, an Ole Miss alumnus, batted .233 with one
homer in 222 games over three years with the New York
Yankees. Won a World Series ring with the Yankees in
1961.

Andy Reese, Tupelo (1904-02-07) 1927
Outfielder/infielder batted .281 with 14 home runs and
111 RBIs in four seasons with the New York Giants. Hit
.308 with six homers and 44 RBIs in 109 games in 1928.

Laddie Renfroe, Natchez (1962-05-09) 1991
Right-hander, an Ole Miss product, posted a 13.50 ERA
in four games (4 2/3 innings) in his one year with the
Chicago Cubs.

Culley Rikard, Oxford (1914-05-09) 1941
Left-handed hitting outfielder batted .270 with four
homers and 37 RBIs in 153 games over three seasons
with Pittsburgh. Served three years (1943-45) in the
Army during World War II.

Jim Roberts, Artesia (1895-10-13) 1924
Right-hander, a Mississippi State alumnus, went 0-3
with a 7.18 ERA in 12 games over two years with
Brooklyn.

Ray Roberts, Cruger (1895-08-25) 1919
Right-hander, who played at Mississippi State, posted an
0-2 mark and a 7.71 ERA in three games for the
Philadelphia A's.

Kevin Rogers, Cleveland (1968-08-20) 1992
Left-hander, a Mississippi Delta Community College
alum, put up a 3.17 ERA in three seasons with San
Francisco. Made 64 of his 79 career appearances in 1993
and finished with a 2.68 ERA.

Nate Rolison, Petal (1977-03-27) 2000
Left-handed hitting first baseman went 1-for-13 with
two RBIs in eight games for Florida in his lone season.

Reb Russell, Jackson (1889-03-12) 1913
Left-hander played nine seasons, seven (1913-19) with
the Chicago White Sox as a pitcher and two (1922-23)
with Pittsburgh as an outfielder. Posted an 80-59 record
with a 2.33 ERA before an arm injury ended his pitching
career. Returned with the Pirates and batted .323 with 21
home runs and 133 RBIs. Given name Ewell Albert.

George Scott, Greenville (1944-03-23) 1966

First baseman/third baseman hit .268 with 271 home runs and 1,051 RBIs in 14 seasons with four American League clubs (Boston, Milwaukee, Kansas City and New York). Three-time All-Star. Eight-time Gold Glove winner at first base. Led the league in homers (36) and RBIs (109) in 1975 with the Brewers. Played in the 1967 World Series with the Red Sox, for whom he played nine years. Nicknamed "Boomer."

John Scott, Jackson (1952-01-24) 1974
Outfielder batted .222 over three seasons with two teams, San Diego and Toronto. Drafted No. 2 overall by the Padres out of a California high school in 1970. Hit .240 with 10 steals in 79 games for the Blue Jays in 1977.

Kim Seaman, Pascagoula (1957-05-06) 1979
Left-hander went 3-2 with a 3.16 ERA and four saves in 27 games over two years with St. Louis.

Pete Shields, Swiftwater (1891-09-21) 1915
First baseman batted .208 in 23 games in his one season with the Cleveland Indians.

*Tony Sipp, Pascagoula (1983-07-12) 2009
Left-hander, a Mississippi Gulf Coast Community College product, posted a 3.43 ERA in 185 games (all in relief) over three seasons with Cleveland. Had a 10-5 record and one save.

Matt Skrmetta, Biloxi (1972-11-06) 2000
Right-hander put up an 11.66 ERA in 14 games in his one year, split between Montreal and Pittsburgh.

Jason Smith, Meridian (1977-07-24) 2001

Left-handed hitting infielder, a Meridian Community College alumnus, played nine seasons for eight different teams, batting .212 with 17 home runs in 278 games. Wore 10 different numbers in the big leagues.

Mike "Mississippi" Smith, Jackson (1961-02-23) 1984
Right-hander, a Utica Junior College product, made 33 appearances over five seasons with three National League teams, Cincinnati, Montreal and Pittsburgh. Posted a 4.71 ERA. Contemporary of Mike "Texas" Smith, also a right-handed pitcher.

*Seth Smith, Jackson (1982-09-30) 2007
Left-handed hitting outfielder, an Ole Miss product, batted .275 with 51 home runs and 181 RBIs in five years with Colorado. Hit .293 with 15 homers in 133 games in 2009, his first full season. Played in the 2007 World Series.

Red Smyth, Holly Springs (1893-01-30) 1915
Left-handed hitting outfielder/second baseman hit .191 in 128 games over four years with Brooklyn and the St. Louis Cardinals.

Homer Spragins, Grenada (1920-11-09) 1947
Right-hander, a Mississippi State alum, pitched in four games (6.75 ERA) for the Philadelphia Phillies.

Dolly Stark, Ripley (1885-01-19) 1909
Second baseman/shortstop, who coached at Mississippi A&M (State) in 1909, batted .238 in 127 games in four seasons with two clubs, Cleveland and Brooklyn. Killed by gunshot on Dec. 1, 1924, in Memphis. Given name Monroe Randolph.

James Steels, Jackson (1961-05-30) 1987

Left-handed hitting outfielder/first baseman hit .180 in 111 games over three years with three clubs, San Diego, Texas and San Francisco.

Blake Stein, McComb (1973-08-03) 1998
Right-hander went 21-28 with a 5.41 ERA in five seasons with Oakland and Kansas City. Posted an 8-5 mark with a 4.68 for the 2000 Royals.

*Taylor Tankersley, Vicksburg (1983-03-07) 2006
Left-hander, a Warren Central High School alum whose birthplace is sometimes listed as Missoula, Mont., made 168 relief appearances over four years with Florida. Put up a 4.58 ERA with eight wins and four saves.

*Craig Tatum, Hattiesburg (1983-03-18) 2009
Catcher, a Mississippi State product, batted .223 with a homer and 22 RBIs in 100 games over three seasons with Cincinnati and Baltimore. Batted .281 for the Orioles in 2010. Drafted in the third round by the Reds in 2004.

Bob Taylor, Leland (1944-03-20) 1970
Left-handed hitting outfielder batted .190 with two home runs in 63 games in one year with San Francisco.

*Marcus Thames, Louisville (1977-03-06) 2002
Outfielder, an East Central Community College alumnus, played 10 seasons with four clubs (New York Yankees, Texas, Detroit and Los Angeles Dodgers) and hit .246 with 115 homers. Totaled 26 homers for the Tigers in 2006 and 25 for the Tigers in 2008.

John Thomson, Vicksburg (1973-10-01) 1997
Right-hander posted a 63-85 record and a 4.68 ERA over 10 seasons with five teams, Colorado, Atlanta, New

York Mets, Texas and Kansas City. Went 14-8 with a 3.72 for the Braves in 2004. Batted .198 in 318 career at-bats.

*Matt Tolbert, McComb (1982-05-04) 2008
Switch-hitting infielder, an Ole Miss alumnus, batted .230 with 54 RBIs in 247 games over four years with Minnesota. Hit .283 in 41 games as a rookie.

Freddie Toliver, Natchez (1961-02-03) 1984
Right-hander had a 10-16 mark with a 4.73 ERA over seven seasons with five teams, Cincinnati, Philadelphia, Minnesota, San Diego and Pittsburgh. Went 7-6 with a 4.24 for the 1988 Twins.

Eddie "Scooter" Tucker, Greenville (1966-11-18) 1992
Catcher, a Delta State product, batted .126 with one homer in 51 games over three years with Houston and Cleveland.

Fred Valentine, Clarksdale (1935-01-19) 1959
Switch-hitting outfielder batted .247 with 36 homers and 138 RBIs in seven seasons with Baltimore and Washington. Hit 16 homers with a .276 average for the Senators in 1966. Nicknamed "Squeaky."

Jermaine Van Buren, Laurel (1980-07-02) 2005
Right-hander made 16 appearances (1-2, 9.00 ERA) over two seasons with the Chicago Cubs and Boston. Drafted in the second round out of Hattiesburg High by Colorado in 1998.

Jonathan Van Every, Brandon (1979-11-27) 2008
Left-handed hitting outfielder, an Itawamba Community College alum, played 40 games over three years with

Boston, batting .211 with two homers. Also pitched in two games.

*Donnie Veal, Jackson (1984-09-18) 2009
Left-hander posted a 7.16 ERA in 19 games (16 1/3 innings) for Pittsburgh in his lone season.

Sammy Vick, Batesville (1895-04-12) 1917
Outfielder, a Millsaps College product, batted .248 in 213 games over five seasons with the New York Yankees and Boston Red Sox.

Chico Walker, Jackson (1957-11-25) 1980
Switch-hitting outfielder/third baseman batted .246 with 17 home runs, 116 RBIs and 67 steals in 11 seasons with four clubs, Boston, Chicago Cubs, California and New York Mets. Hit .257 with six homers and 13 steals in 124 games for the '91 Cubs. Given name Cleotha.

Gerald "Gee" Walker, Gulfport (1908-03-19) 1931
Outfielder, an Ole Miss product, hit .294 with 124 homers, 997 RBIs and 223 stolen bases over 15 seasons. Played for five different teams: Detroit, Chicago White Sox, Washington, Cleveland and Cincinnati. Appeared in one All-Star Game and two World Series, winning a ring with Detroit in 1935. Hit .335 with 18 homers, 113 RBIs and 23 steals for the Tigers in 1937.

Harry Walker, Pascagoula (1916-10-22) 1940
Left-handed hitting outfielder batted .296 in 807 games over 11 seasons with four National League clubs, St. Louis, Philadelphia, Cincinnati and Chicago. Did two years of military service (1944-45) in mid-career. Won a batting title in 1947, hitting .363 for the Cardinals. Played in two All-Star Games and three World Series, winning rings with the Cardinals in 1942 and '46. Also

managed nine years in the majors. Nicknamed "The Hat."

Hub Walker, Gulfport (1906-08-17) 1931
Left-handed hitting outfielder, an Ole Miss alumnus, batted .263 in 297 games over five seasons with Cincinnati and Detroit. Served three years in the Navy during World War II. Didn't play in the majors from 1938-44, then won a World Series ring with the Tigers in 1945. Given name Harvey Willos. Brother of Gee Walker.

Fred Walters, Laurel (1912-09-04) 1945
Catcher, a Mississippi State alum, hit .172 in 40 games in his one season with the Boston Red Sox.

Herb Washington, Belzoni (1951-11-16) 1974
Pinch runner, who never batted in the majors, stole 31 bases and scored 33 runs in two years (105 games) with Oakland. Appeared in the 1974 World Series. Won an NCAA sprint championship at Michigan State.

Fred Waters, Benton (1927-02-02) 1955
Left-hander, a Southern Miss product, posted a 2-2 mark with a 2.89 ERA in 25 games over two years with Pittsburgh.

Skeeter Webb, Meridian (1909-11-04) 1932
Shortstop/second baseman, an Ole Miss alumnus, played in 699 games over 12 seasons, batting .219. Debuted with the St. Louis Cardinals in 1932, then didn't appear in another big league game until 1938. Also played for Cleveland, Chicago White Sox, Detroit and Philadelphia A's. Given name James Laverne.

Barry Wesson, Tupelo (1977-04-06) 2002

Outfielder batted .194 with one home run in 25 games over two seasons with Houston and Anaheim.

Frank White, Greenville (1950-09-04) 1973
Second baseman batted .255 with 160 homers, 886 RBIs and 178 stolen bases in 18 seasons, all with Kansas City. Hit .298 with 45 doubles, 11 homers and 56 RBIs for the 1982 Royals. Five-time All-Star. Eight-time Gold Glove winner. Appeared in two World Series, winning a ring in 1985.

*Eli Whiteside, New Albany (1979-10-22) 2005
Catcher, a Delta State product, played four years with Baltimore and San Francisco, batting .218 with four homers and 10 RBIs in 196 games. Won a World Series ring with the Giants in 2010.

Papa Williams, Meridian (1913-07-17) 1945
First baseman hit .211 in 19 at-bats for Cleveland in his one season. Given name Fred.

Doc Wood, Batesville (1900-02-28) 1923
Shortstop, an Ole Miss product, went 1-for-3 in three games for the Philadelphia A's. Given name Charles Spencer.

Dmitri Young, Vicksburg (1973-10-11) 1996
Switch-hitter, who played outfield, first and third base, batted .298 with 171 homers and 683 RBIs over 13 seasons with four clubs, St. Louis, Cincinnati, Detroit and Washington. Hit 29 homers for the Tigers in 2003. Two-time All-Star. Fourth overall pick by the Cardinals in 1991 out of a California high school.

Pete Young, Meadville (1968-03-19) 1992

Right-hander, a Mississippi State alumnus, went 1-0 with a 3.86 ERA in 17 games over two seasons with Montreal. Sixth-round draft pick by the Expos in 1992.

Tim Young, Gulfport (1973-10-15) 1998
Left-hander posted a 6.23 ERA in 18 games over two seasons, one each with Montreal and Boston.

Walter Young, Hattiesburg (1980-02-18) 2005
Left-handed hitting first baseman batted .303 with one home run in 33 at-bats for Pittsburgh in his one season. Listed at 6 feet 5, 320 pounds, one of the heaviest players in big league history.

Acknowledgements

Thanks to my wife, Susan, and kids Kelly and Marshall for their encouragement and support and also to Susan Puckett, Alan Huffman, Rick Cleveland, Joe Powell, T. Scott Brandon, Phillip Wellman, the late Gene Wiggins, the late Art Kaul and all my press box buddies over the years from Smith-Wills Stadium and Trustmark Park.

Bibliography

Adomites, Paul, *October's Game*. Alexandria, Va.: Redefintion, Inc., 1990

Alexander, Charles C., Our Game. New York: Henry Holt and Co., 1991

Anderson, Dave, *Pennant Races*. New York: Doubleday, 1994

Associated Press

The Ballplayers (Mike Shatzkin, ed.). New York: Harbor House/William Morrow and Co., 1990

Barber, Red, *1947: When All Hell Broke Loose in Baseball*. Garden City, N.Y.: Doubleday and Co., 1982

Baseball America

BaseballLibrary.com

Baseball's Unforgettable Games (Joe Reichler and Ben Olan, eds.) New York: The Ronald Press Co., 1960

Boston, Talmadge, *1939: Baseball's Pivotal Year*. Fort Worth, Texas: The Summit Group, 1994

Boswell, Thomas, *Why Time Begins on Opening Day*. New York: Penguin Books, 1984

Cattau, Daniel, "So maybe there really is such a thing as 'the natural,'" *Smithsonian Magazine*, July 1991

The Clarion-Ledger (Jackson, Miss.)

Cohen, Stanley, *Dodgers! The First 100 Years*. New York: Carol Publishing Group, 1990

The Commercial Appeal (Memphis)

Craft, David, *The Negro Le*agues. New York: Crescent Books, 1993

Creamer, Robert W., *Baseball in '41*. New York: Penguin Books, 1991

Creamer, Robert W. (with Red Barber), Rhubarb in the Catbird Seat. Garden City, N.Y.: Doubleday and Co., Inc., 1968

Edwards, Bob. *Fridays with Red*. New York: Simon and Schuster, 1993

The Encyclopedia of Minor League Baseball (Lloyd Johnson and Miles Wolff, eds.) Durham, N.C.: Baseball America Inc., 1993

ESPNLosAngeles.com

Falkner, David, "6-4-3," The Sporting News, Aug. 14, 1995

Fimrite, Ron, "Good to the Very Last Out," Sports Illustrated, Nov. 3, 1986

Gregory, Robert, *DIZ: The Story of Dizzy Dean and Baseball During the Great Depression*. New York: Penguin Books/Viking Press, 1992

Hanks, Stephen, *150 Years of Baseball*. Lincolnwood, Ill.: Publications International, Ltd., 1989

Hetrick, J. Thomas, *Misfits: The Cleveland Spiders in 1899.* Jefferson, N.C., and London: McFarland and Co., Inc., Publishers, 1991

Holway, John B., *The Sluggers*. Alexandria, Va.: Redefinition, Inc., 1989

Honig, Donald, *Baseball Between the Lines*. Lincoln, Neb.: University of Nebraska Press, 1976

Honig, Donald, *Baseball: When the Grass Was Real*. New York: Coward, McCann and Geoghegan, Inc. 1975

Hoppel, Joe, *The Series*. St. Louis, Mo.: The Sporting News Publishing Co., 1992

Houston Chronicle

James, Bill, *The Historical Baseball Abstract*. New York: Free Press, 2001

James, Bill, *This Time Let's Not Eat the Bones*. New York: Villard Books, 1989

Johnson, Lloyd, *Baseball's Dream Teams*. New York: Gallery Books/W.H. Smith Publishers Inc., 1990

Kansas City Star

Kavanagh, Gerard, "Frank White: Good as Gold." Street and Smith's Baseball Yearbook 1989

Kerrane, Kevin, *The Hurlers*. Alexandria, Va.:
Redefintion, Inc., 1989

Kram, Mark, "No Place in the Shade," *Sports
Illustrated*, June 20,
1994 (reprinted from 1973)

Kuenster, Bob, "Some Memorable At-Bats by Star
Players," *Baseball Digest,* June 1994

Lidz, Franz, "Whatever Happened to ... Herb
Washington," *Sports Illustrated*, July 19, 1993

Lieb, Frederick G., *The Detroit Tigers*. New York:
G.P. Putnam's Sons, 1946

Lindberg, Richard, *Who's on Third?* South Bend, Ind.:
Icarus Press, 1983

Lowry, Philip J., *Green Cathedrals*. Reading, Mass.:
Addison-Wesley Publishing Co., Inc., 1992

Mead, William B., *Low and Outside*. Alexandria, Va.:
Redefinition, Inc., 1990

Mead, William B., *The Explosive Sixties*. Alexandria,
Va.: Redefinition, Inc., 1989

Mississippi Sports Legends (published by the
Mississippi Sports Foundation, Inc., Jackson), Vol. 1,
No. 1, Winter 1994

Nack, William, "George Scott is Alive and Well and Playing in Mexico City," *Sports Illustrated*, Aug. 17, 1981

Nemec, David, *The Rules of Baseball*. New York: Lyons and Burford Publishers, 1994

Neyer, Rob and Eddie Epstein, *Baseball Dynasties: The Greatest Teams of All Time*. New York: W.W. Norton and Company, 2000

Olson, Stan, "Bobby Richardson Looks Back on the Yankee Dynasty Years," *Baseball Digest*, September 1995

Peterson, Robert, *Only the Ball Was White*. New York: McGraw-Hill Book Co., 1984 (originally published in 1970)

Reichler, Joseph, *Baseball's Greatest Moments*. New York: A Rutledge Book/Bonanza Books, 1985

Reynolds, Bill, *Lost Summer*. New York: Warner Books, Inc. 1992

Rieland, Randy, The New Professionals. Alexandria, Va.: Redefinition, Inc., 1989

Riley, James A., *The Biographical Encyclopedia of the Negro Leagues*. New York: Carroll and Graf Publishers, Inc., 1994

Ritter, Lawrence, *The Glory of Their Times.* New York: McMillan, 1966

Ritter, Lawrence and Donald Honig, *The Image of Their Greatness.* New York: Crown Publishers, Inc., 1984 (originally published in 1979)

Ritter, Lawrence, *Lost Ballparks.* New York: Penguin Books, 1992

Rogosin, Donn, *Invisible Men.* New York: Kodansha International, 1995 (originally published in 1983)

Rust, Art Jr., *Get That Nigger off the Field.* New York: Delacorte Press, 1976

Shutt, Timothy Baker, "When Baseball Came Home from the War," *Sports History*, July 1987

Smith, Ken, "Rifle-Armed Outfielders," Street and Smith's Baseball Yearbook 1979

The Sports Encyclopedia: Baseball (David Neft and Richard Cohen, eds.). New York: St. Martin's Press, 1992

Swift, E.M., "The Can's a New Man," *Sports Illustrated*, June 3, 1991

Tygiel, Jules, *Baseball's Great Experiment.* New York: Oxford University Press, 1983

USA Today

Van Blair, Rick, "Harry Danning: Catching Star of Another Era," *Baseball Digest,* October 1994

Verducci, Tom, "A Farewell to Skinny Arms," Inside Baseball. New York: A Sports Illustrated Book/Time Inc., 2006

Verducci, Tom, "Totally Juiced," *Inside Baseball*. New York: A Sports Illustrated Book/Time Inc., 2006

Wagenheim, Kal, *Babe Ruth: His Life and Legend.* New York: An Owl Book/Henry Holt and Co., 1992 (originally published in 1974)

Ward, Geoffrey and Ken Burns, *Baseball: An Illustrated History*. New York: Alfred A. Knopf, 1994

"When Ol' Luke Easter Hit 'Em, He Really Hit 'Em," *Baseball Digest*, April 1994

ABOUT THE AUTHOR

Mike Christensen was born in Illinois and grew up in Augusta, Georgia. A graduate of the University of Georgia with a master's degree from the University of Southern Mississippi, he was a newspaper sports writer/copy editor for 30 years. He now works as an editor/writer for AgFax.com, an agriculture information site. He continues to do free-lance sports writing and blogs about baseball at allmississippibaseball.net.

www.ingramcontent.com/pod-product-compliance
Lightning Source LLC
Chambersburg PA
CBHW072342090426
42741CB00012B/2887